WHEN THE APPLE RIPENS

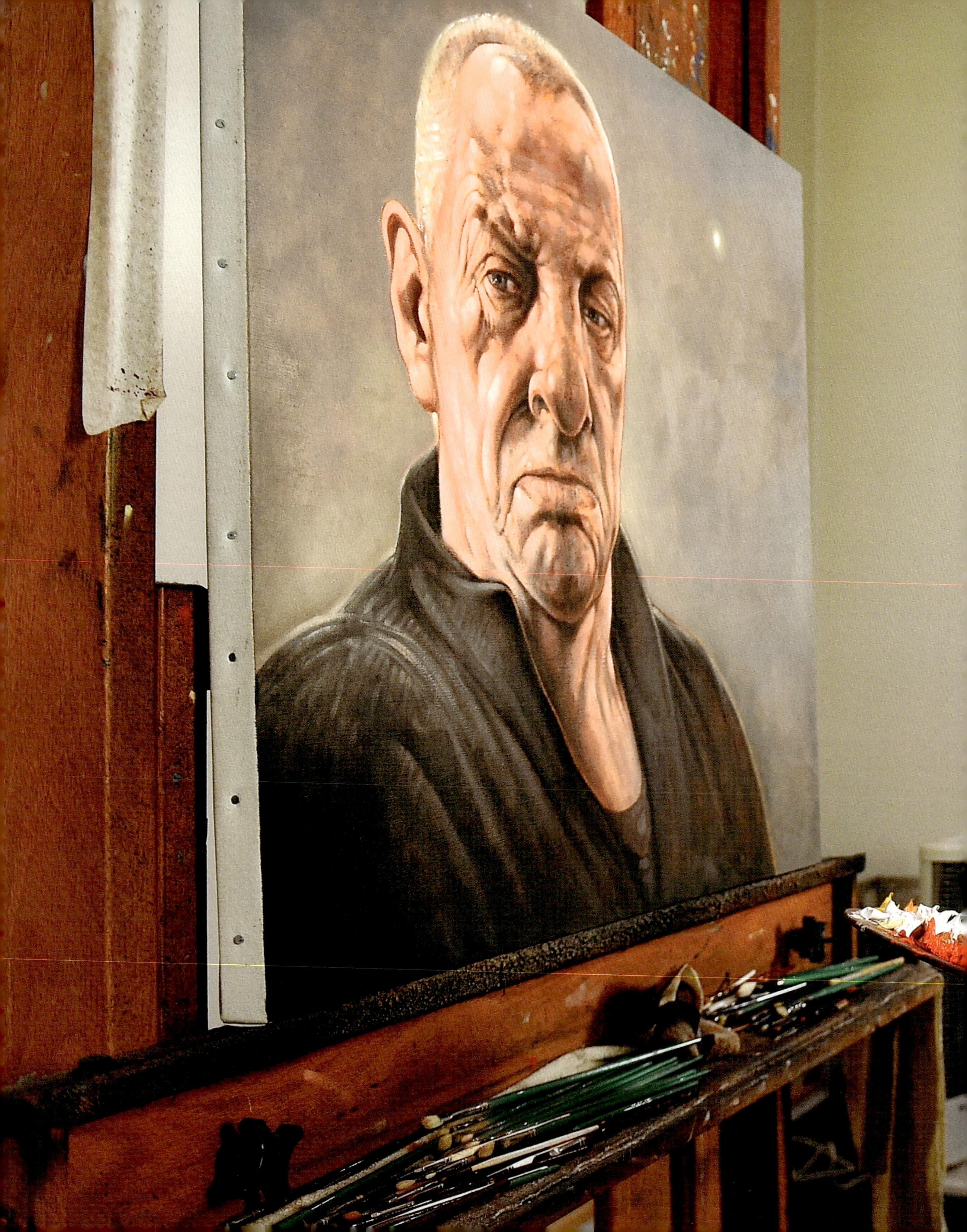

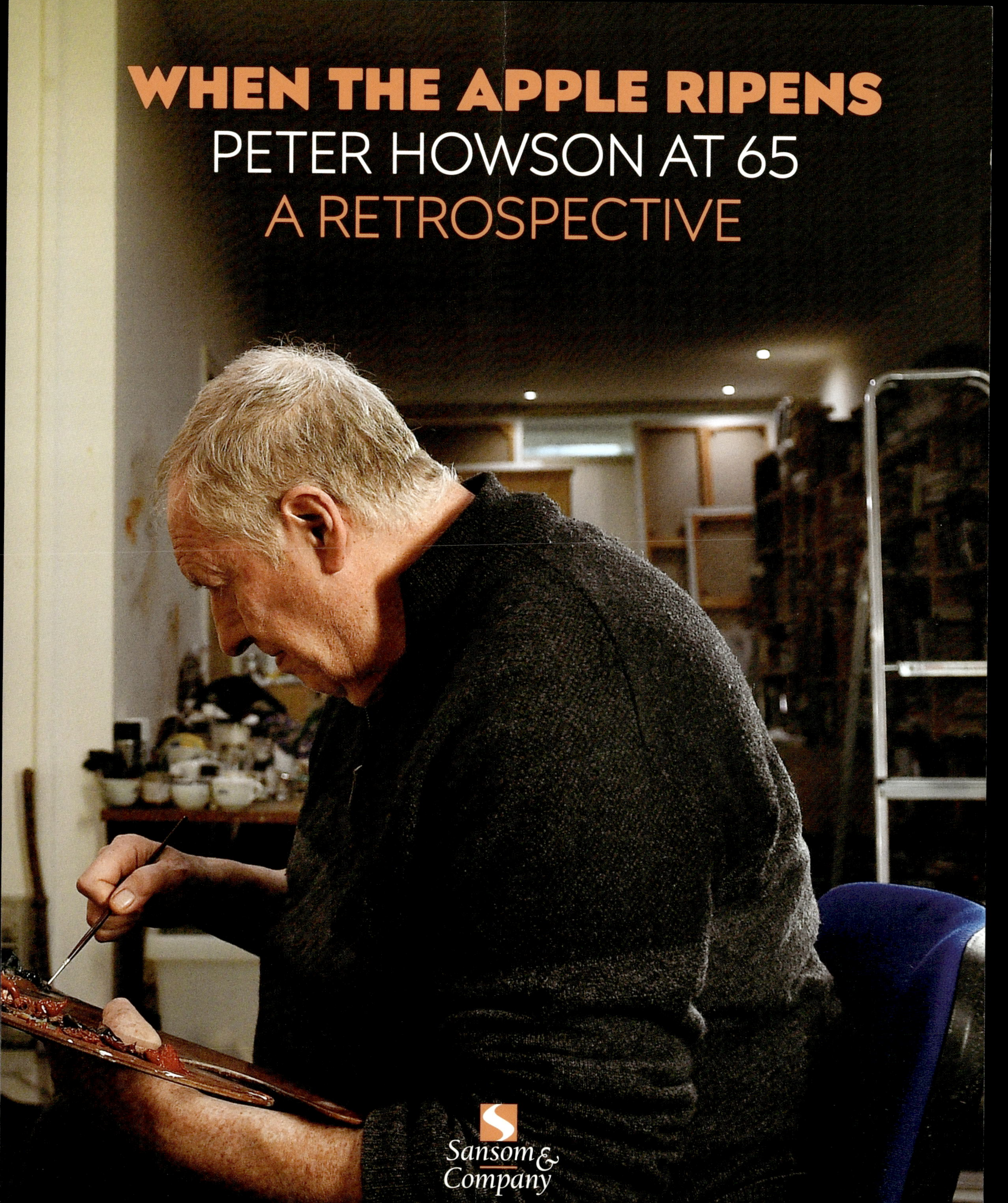

WHEN THE APPLE RIPENS
PETER HOWSON AT 65
A RETROSPECTIVE
Sansom &
Company

**I dedicate this book and retrospective to Angela Flowers,
whose kindness and support I will never forget.**
Peter Howson

First published in 2023 by Sansom & Company,
a publishing imprint of Redcliffe Press Ltd,
81G Pembroke Road, Bristol BS8 3EA
www.sansomandcompany.co.uk / info@sansomandcompany.co.uk

Published on the occasion of the exhibition
When the Apple Ripens: Peter Howson at 65: A Retrospective
City Art Centre, Edinburgh, 27 May–1 October 2023

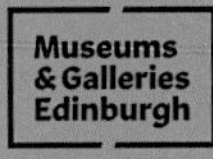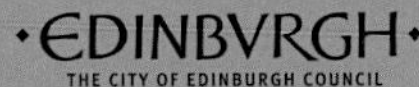

ISBN 978-1-915670-05-2

British Library Cataloguing-in-Publication Data
A catalogue record for this book is available from the British Library.

Commissioning editor Paul Deaton
Copyediting Ann Kay
Design and typesetting E&P Design
Printed and bound by Akcent Media

This book is made from Forest Stewardship Council® certified paper.
Sansom & Company is committed to being an environmentally friendly publisher.

Front cover
Trinity (detail) / **2022** / **oil on canvas** / **183 x 153cm** / photograph Antonio Parente

Back cover and frontispiece
Peter Howson, 2023 / photographs Greg McVean

For further information
peterhowson.co.uk
flowersgallery.com

CONTENTS

FOREWORD

Along with many others, I had followed the roller-coaster career of Peter Howson in the media before ever meeting the artist face to face. Initially it was his meteoric rise after art school, when his paintings and those of his Glasgow School of Art contemporaries were being purchased by major international museums. Then came Bosnia. The raw brutishness of those early works made him the ideal choice as an official war artist, sent to try and record a country being torn apart.

The press back home relished the stories of Peter's struggles as he sought to come to terms with the atrocities meted out by both sides in the conflict. This was a war in which neighbour turned against neighbour, where the fighting was hand-to-hand, up close, and deadly. The actual numbers of casualties are still contested, but independent studies have concluded that around 100,000 civilians were killed and more than 2 million people displaced. How could anyone who hadn't been battle-hardened as a soldier process what he saw with his own eyes?

Peter's subsequent turmoil, in both his personal and professional lives, was played out in various articles in the newspapers and on television. Quite understandably he withdrew from public life, cautious of others who might seek to take further advantage.

It was in such a period that I first met him. I'd been asked to curate an exhibition for the City Art Centre in Edinburgh on the theme of Saint Andrew, Scotland's Patron Saint, born out of the great deal of political interest from the Nationalist community in making Saint Andrew's Day a public holiday in Scotland. It was suggested to me that we might commission a contemporary artist to tackle the subject and I proposed that an approach to Peter should be made.

I'd been advised that because of his Asperger's Peter would only have a limited time to speak to me. Along with a colleague, we laid out before him where our research had taken us and put forward the proposal of a new work about the Saint. We left not knowing what his reaction would be. Over a month went by without any contact, so I tentatively made the call assuming the silence inferred a rejection. Imagine the surprise when I was told that not only had Peter accepted the proposal, but he'd already been to Israel with a film crew in a bid to immerse himself in the places and environments where Jesus's disciple had walked.

The project consumed him for the subsequent months, and we ended up abandoning the idea of a multidisciplinary historical exhibition in favour of a one-person show. During the run-up to the exhibition, I got to know the artist a little bit better. I came to appreciate his immense talent and total dedication to his work, and to better understand his view of the world.

At the time of the Saint Andrew exhibition in 2006, the City of Edinburgh's art collection contained two works by Howson – *Regimental Bath* (p. 31), a powerful, disturbing picture of sadistic bullying from his army days, and a wonderful woodcut entitled *The Noble Dosser*. The exhibition gave us the opportunity to add a few others, chosen to show Peter's consummate skill in different media.

This retrospective exhibition comes on the occasion of Peter's sixty-fifth birthday. Exhibitions of this scale are always team efforts. On behalf of the City Art Centre, I'd like to pay special tribute to Matthew Flowers and his team at Flowers Gallery in London. They have represented Peter from the 1980s, through the ups and downs, and Matthew's thoughtful advice, his patience with my many emails, and his introductions to collectors have been instrumental in putting the show together. Stan Bethwaite, Peter's Studio and Business Manager, also deserves special mention. Stan has followed up my enquiries, liaised with Peter when decisions must be made, and has always been ready to help.

I'd like to offer a special thank you to the many public and private lenders involved with the exhibition. Through their generosity we have been allowed the privilege of assembling in one display paintings which normally take pride of place in their homes, offices, galleries and museums. Their support is greatly appreciated.

Finally, to Peter himself. Always generous with his time when we meet, totally involved in the project from the first chat, eager to help where he can. And all the time working on the next painting or drawing, still pushing the boundaries, still attempting new things.

David Patterson
Curatorial and Conservation Manager
Edinburgh Museums and Galleries

BETWEEN HEAVEN AND HELL
APPROACHING THE LATER WORK

Susan Mansfield

When Peter Howson was 12 years old, he became convinced that the world was about to end. It would end in a year, he believed, and he was at least half-excited by the prospect. In the interim, he would make a drawing every month, inspired by the scenes of judgement and apocalypse he had found in the Book of Revelation.

Those drawings are now lost, but the eschatological theme has persisted through Howson's oeuvre, emerging with renewed vigour in recent years. Approaching it with all the technical accomplishment of a mature artist, and with a lifetime's accumulated knowledge of philosophy and religion, literature and art, it is not only his subject but has become a visual language by which he addresses other subjects.

Peter Howson's life and career before 2000 are well documented: his swift rise to fame in the 1980s with vigorous narrative paintings of tramps and boxers, hard-men and hooligans (for example 1989's *Psycho Squad*, overleaf); his experiences as an official war artist in Bosnia, and the harrowing work they gave rise to. The story of the two decades post-2000 is less well known, and much of the work, being made to commission or quickly sold into private collections, has not been shown in public galleries. Studying these paintings, one becomes aware of some continuity with his earlier work, but also that he has struck out in new directions, developing both what I would call his traditional religious painting and his multifaceted apocalyptic visions, and these will be addressed later in some detail. In part due to the lack of public visibility, these achievements – often made against a backdrop of great personal struggle – have been underacknowledged.

Robert Heller has written that 'the autobiographical principle unifies almost all [Howson's] art'.[1] This is not to say that the art is indivisible from the life, but it is important to consider both, as far as they shed light on one another. In providing a context in which the work after 2000 can be understood, it is worth spending some time recapping his story from the beginning.

Peter Howson was born in 1958 in Isleworth, West London, moving with his parents to Prestwick in Scotland at the age of four when his father took up a new post with Air Canada. By his own account, he was an introspective, anxious child who loved drawing. His precocious talent was encouraged by the adults in his life – his first box of oil paints was a gift from his grandmother – but helped make him a target for daily bullying at school. He believes the seam of violence which runs throughout his work has its roots in that experience.

In 1975, at the age of 17 and with a bulging portfolio, he was accepted into Glasgow School of Art. However, he quickly became disillusioned with the restrictions of the traditional training and failed his first year. One day, in second year, as the class waited for a tardy life model, he and a friend left the art school and walked into town, where they joined the army.

In one sense, it was the fulfilment of a lifelong ambition. As a child, Howson had drawn pictures of famous battles and told his parents he wanted to be both a soldier and an artist. However, no sooner had he been assigned to the Royal Highland Fusiliers than he realised he had made a terrible mistake. He resented the authoritarian environment and, although he wasn't bullied himself, witnessed levels of bullying and humiliation which put his school experiences in the shade. Nine months in uniform, including a period of secondment to the elite Scottish Divisional Squad, did nothing to change his mind. Back on civvy street, he took a job as a warehouse manager for a supermarket, and then as a bouncer in a nightclub. He also joined a gym and became a body-builder.

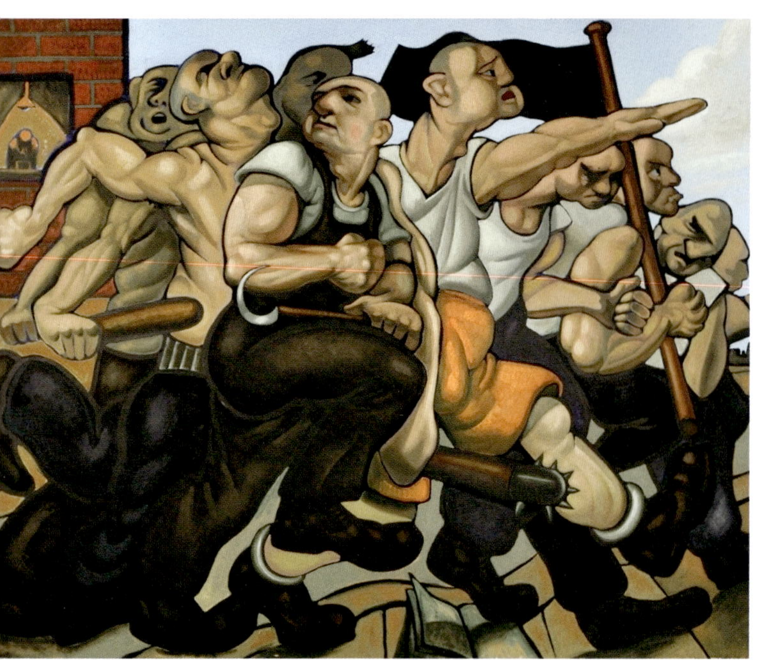

Psycho Squad
1989 / oil on canvas / 210 x 280 cm
private collection / photograph Antonio Parente

By 1979, he was back at Glasgow School of Art, finding a supporter in Sandy Moffat, who had recently joined the teaching staff in the painting department. After seeing some drawings he had done in the army, Moffat encouraged Howson in his choice of narrative, figurative painting, encouraging him to explore its potential to address big social and political issues.[2]

It was Moffat who first brought Howson together with Ken Currie, Adrian Wiszniewski and Steven Campbell in the exhibition *New Image Glasgow* at the Third Eye Centre in 1985. The 'New Glasgow Boys' were not exact contemporaries, but together they garnered widespread attention. The show transferred to London and inspired the exhibition *The Vigorous Imagination* at the Scottish National Gallery of Modern Art in Edinburgh in 1987. The young figurative painters from Glasgow all advanced quickly in their careers. In 1986, aged 28, Howson was taken on by London gallerists Angela and Matthew Flowers.

By the mid-1980s, Howson had found his voice as an artist. He had long been drawn to the people on the fringes of city life; in his final year at art school, he took long walks deep into Glasgow's East End. In 1984, after a short, disastrous marriage, he was living out of his studio in the Gallowgate, in a neighbourhood full of drunks and dossers, gangsters and prostitutes. A soup kitchen next door fed the homeless. All of this fed Howson's work.

His confident, large-scale paintings endowed these characters from the margins with a kind of nobility. In *The Heroic Dosser* (1987, facing page), the tramp seems to tower above us, his hands gripping a railing, perhaps on a sea wall. Light swirls behind him and around a single towering edifice, an empty warehouse or factory. His face is mainly in shadow, but light catches his cheekbone and swept-back hair – part down-and-out in a battered coat,

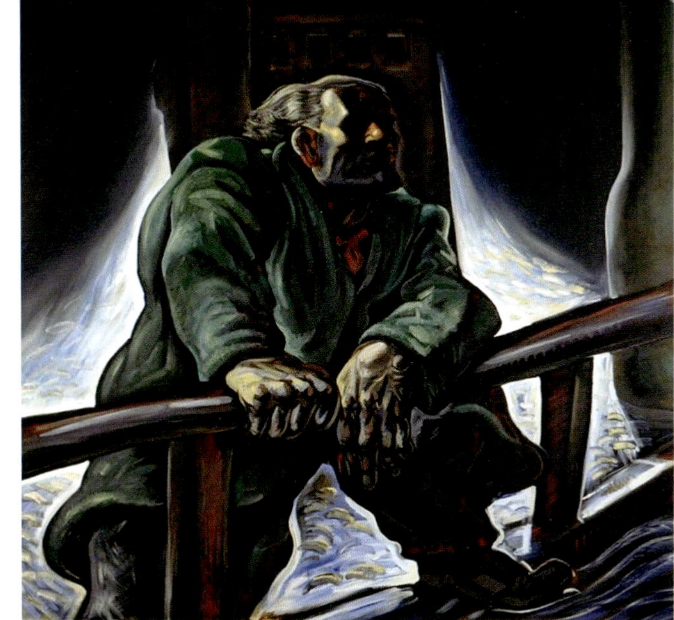

The Heroic Dosser
1987 / oil on canvas / 197.5 x 214 cm
National Galleries of Scotland / presented anonymously through the
British American Arts Association, 1989 / photograph Antonia Reeve

part Caspar David Friedrich's *Wanderer above the Sea of Fog* (c.1817). In paintings of boxers, like *Madai* (1987) and *Blind Leading the Blind VI (Boxer)* (1991, p. 40), Howson portrayed the bulked-up bodies he would have seen in the gym with a fierce pathos: men past their prime who have lost more fights than they won, broken but defiant.

However, his attitude to violence has always been ambivalent. It energises him as much as it repels him. He revisited the brutality he witnessed in the army in paintings like *Regimental Bath* (1985, p. 31) and painted the everyday violence he witnessed in the East End: the street fighters and football hooligans. He was particularly interested when ideologies were involved. In *Patriots* (1991, p. 13), he depicted a surging trio of figures in white vests and red baseball caps. One hefts a broken bottle; pitbull terriers bare their teeth. These dramas were also played out in larger crowd scenes, such as *Death of Innocence* (1989), where the hooligans, in white hats this time, each with a hand raised in a Nazi salute, lead a baying mob which taunts a man who is tied to a tree.

Howson was employing the language of history painting – its dramatic lighting and complex compositions – to depict ugly modern realities. His reference points were Goya, Brueghel, Hieronymus Bosch. He was uninterested in realism and rarely painted from life, preferring to use his intuitive grasp of anatomy to distort and exaggerate aspects of the human figure for dramatic effect. But he was aware – as were his critics – that this approach had its dangers. Howson is a consummate draughtsman, and a tension runs through his work between painting and drawing. To lose control of distortion and exaggeration is to allow the picture to topple over into caricature.

He was ambitious and productive and the work sold well. Glasgow was a post-industrial wasteland in the mid-1980s, on the fringes of Thatcher's Britain, but Howson's larger-than-life pictures of the dispossessed were fetching high prices. His work was shown internationally by Flowers and he was making a lot of money. He met celebrity collectors, jetted around on Concorde, stayed in top hotels. He bought a town house in the West End of Glasgow and developed a drug habit. The Scottish press followed his every move. He told Robert Heller: 'The more the money flowed in, the more the fame came, the less I was able to handle it.'[3] Fearing the money would run out, he would return to his studio after drink- and drug-fuelled binges to paint feverishly through the night.

In 1993, at the age of 35, he was the subject of a major retrospective at Glasgow's McLellan Galleries. Howson was now married, and he and his wife Terry had a small daughter, Lucie. The show was successful, but he was unhappy. Reflecting on this moment some years later, he suggested it was because he had exhausted the subject matter of Glasgow and needed fresh inspiration.[4] At this very moment, an opportunity arose to be considered to go to Bosnia as an official war artist, and Howson seized on it like a lifeline. He understood that war was a key subject for him, and this offered the chance to witness first hand a conflict of almost medieval brutality happening in contemporary Europe.

The details of Howson's two trips to Bosnia in May and November 1993 are well documented, not least because his travel was sponsored by a newspaper and he was being shadowed by a film crew making a BBC documentary. From the outset, he knew what he wanted to do. He was not interested in painting the activities of the British peacekeeping forces. He wanted to get to the essence of the war, to the heart of the brutality played out by neighbour against neighbour. And he did.

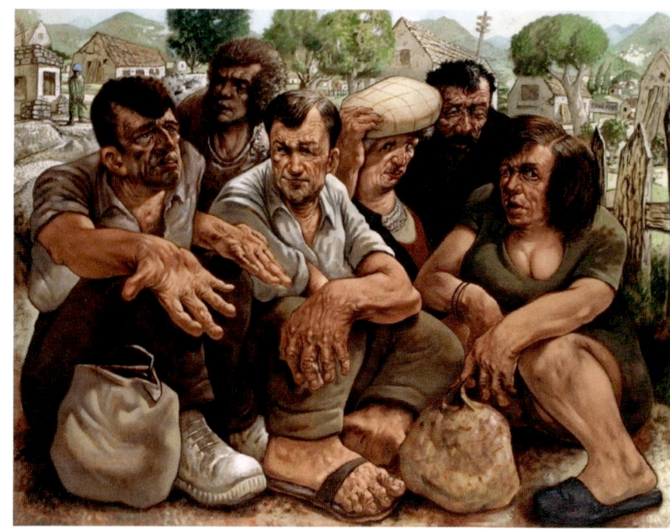

Cleansed
1994 / oil on canvas / 183 x 244 cm
Imperial War Museum, London

Some three hundred works were shown at an exhibition – *Bosnia* – in London the following year, at the Imperial War Museum and in parallel at Flowers East. There was controversy among the purchasing panel at the Imperial War Museum over *Croatian and Muslim* (1994), which depicts a woman being raped in her home while another man forces her head down into a toilet bowl.[5] The painting was eventually purchased by David Bowie. *Plum Grove* (1994), which was bought by the Tate, shows children playing next to the castrated body of a man hanged on a tree branch; a small boy stares at it in fascinated horror. *Road to Zenica* (1994) depicts the ghostly, traumatised faces of refugees, the adults numb, the children animated, maniacal. *Cleansed* (1994, above), which was purchased by the Imperial War Museum, is a restrained composition: a group of displaced Muslims hunkered by a roadside, each worried face telling a story.

There was criticism from some quarters that Howson painted events in Bosnia which he did not personally witness.[6] Robert Crampton writes:

> Truth be told, Howson did not see very much in Bosnia with his eyes. Nobody does. He did not get to Tuzla, or Sarajevo, or Mostar. He plodded around and found out that war is hell, war is frightening, war is boring, war is hard … But the truth is, women do get raped in war, men do get castrated, children do turn into monsters. And Howson has seen it after all in his imagination, and all too vividly. We all have. Wouldn't he be untruthful if he did not paint it? Someone has to.[7]

However, this came at great personal cost. For several months after his return from Bosnia, Howson could not paint at all. He was traumatised by what he had seen, and what he had been forced to imagine. His marriage to Terry ended, and he moved from Glasgow to London. He recognised this, with hindsight, as deep depression – a harbinger, perhaps, that there was worse to come. However, at the same time, his work was reinvigorated. Bosnia had given him 'more material than the whole of the past 15 years of being in Glasgow'.[8]

With the opening of *Bosnia* at the Imperial War Museum in September 1994, the dark clouds lifted. Bosnia, he said, had given him a new perspective on life; he was no longer interested in money. Installed in a new studio in Hackney, he explored his feelings about the end of his marriage and separation from his daughter in 'The Rake's Progress' series (see *My Tale Shall Be Told*, 1995, p. 14), which some critics described as his best work to date.[9] In 1997, Alan Jackson described him as a man who had 'achieved something approaching content-ment'.[10] Work was going well. Some of his Bosnia paintings had been included in a show of war art at Galerie Piltzer in Paris, alongside work by his heroes, Otto Dix and Goya. Matthew Flowers described him as 'a very serious artist – a very serious man. The best', he said, 'is yet to come.'[11]

¶

Would that any human life could be told simply as a narrative of progress, in which difficulties are always overcome and lessons always learned. This is the point at which it becomes impossible to fit the story of Peter Howson to this form. At the end of the 1990s, he was back in the East End of Glasgow and was struggling, joining an aid convoy to Kosovo in 1999 'almost to run away from my life'.[12] In November 2000, he collapsed and was admitted to Castle Craig near Peebles to be treated for drug and alcohol addiction. There, while following Alcoholics Anonymous's 12-step programme, he converted to the Christian faith.

He left Castle Craig sober, drug-free and with a new-found faith, but this is not a simple story of a transformed life, a new beginning. While his faith never left him, the years to come would bring relapses and breakdowns, long stays in psychiatric hospitals and over-confident proclamations of recovery, each of which seemed to be followed by a further crash more painful than the one before. He told an interviewer in 2013: 'So it's been up and down all the time, being ill, being well, being hyper, being depressed.'[13]

In a wide-ranging book referencing artists, writers and composers, American psychologist Kay Redfield Jamison explores the link between mood disorders – specifically 'manic depression' (now termed bipolar disorder) – and the artistic temperament, find-ing 'a compelling association, not to say actual overlap'[14] between the two. In one study in which she interviewed 47 eminent British artists, playwrights, poets, novelists and biographers, she found that 38 per cent had been treated for a mood disorder, evidence for a 'strong association between mood disorders and creativity'.[15] She also notes a correspondence between mood disorders and alcohol and drug dependencies. She writes:

> The fiery aspects of thought and feeling that initially compel the artistic voyage – fierce energy, high mood, and quick intelligence; a sense of the visionary and the grand; a restless and feverish temperament – commonly carry with them the capacity for vastly darker moods, grimmer energies, and, occasionally, bouts of 'madness'.[16]

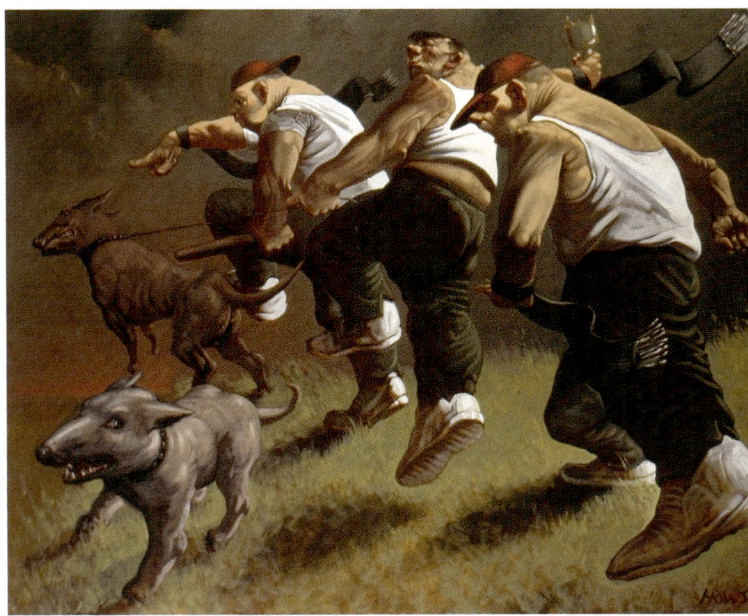

Patriots
1991 / oil on canvas / 206 x 274.5 cm
Glasgow Life Museums

Drawing on documentation of the lives of artistic figures including Robert Lowell, William Cowper, Vincent van Gogh, Robert Schumann and Virginia Woolf, she argues that 'positive features associated with certain kinds of madness ... might, in some instances, combine with other talents to produce an extraordinarily creative or accomplished person.'[17] Indeed, she argues that sometimes highly accomplished people are diagnosed 'melancholic' rather than manic-depressive, because the 'manic' (now 'mania') phase of the illness manifests as energised, productive creativity.[18]

At the same time, Jamison emphasises that sustained creative output requires high levels of discipline, control and rationality, typically when the person is 'well', and points out that many of those whom she studied described their creative work as the best way to regulate their moods.[19] The eighteenth-century English poet William Cowper wrote: 'Dejection of Spirits, which I suppose may have prevented many a man from becoming an Author, made me one. I find constant employment necessary, and therefore take care to be constantly employed.'[20] Peter Howson says, simply: 'Work is the only thing that keeps me level.'

There is another reason to take 2000 as the starting point for a discussion of Howson's more recent art, and that is the seminal importance of his Christian conversion. Of course, Christian ideas and imagery were already present in his work. He was taken to church as a child, and painted a vivid crucifixion at the age of six. He read the book of Revelation as a teenager. In 1996, he talked to Alan Jackson about 'reconnecting to God',[21] and painted a tender portrait of Christ in 1998 (*Man of Sorrows*). But following his personal encounter with God in Castle Craig, there was a more deliberate

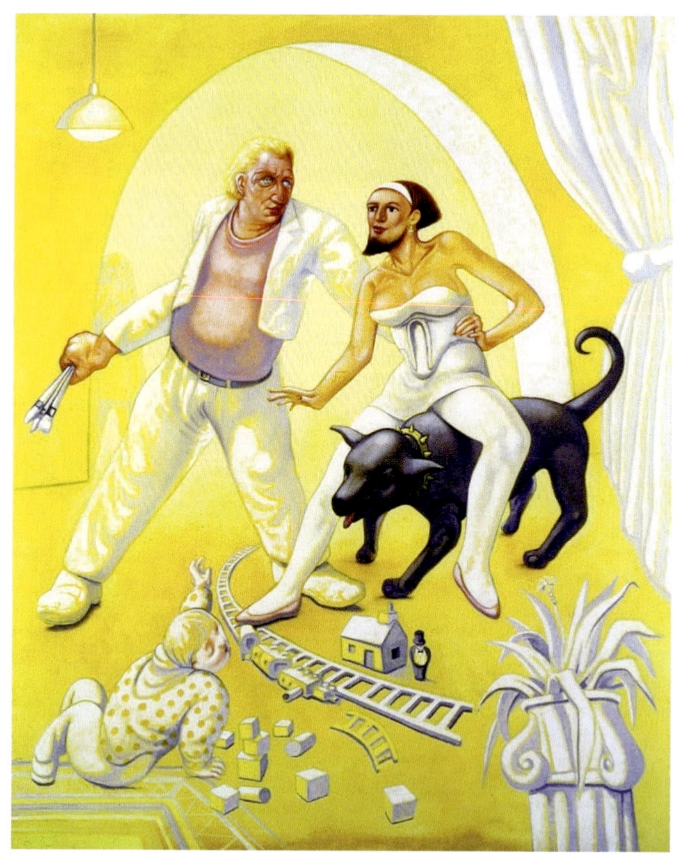

My Tale Shall Be Told from 'The Rake's Progress' series
1995 / oil on canvas / 152.5 x 122 cm
Flowers Gallery / photograph Antonio Parente

turn towards religious subject matter, and to using a visual language drawn from religion to address other subjects.

As Caleb Froehlich has written, there is a danger that Howson's conversion has not been taken seriously, either as a personal life-changing event or for its impact on his visual language.[22] In the art world of the twenty-first century, faith is hardly fashionable. John A. Kohan puts it like this:

> In the age of cool, when we study art with ironic detachment and make up our own stories about what we see, Howson insists that the meaning of his passion-filled paintings can be found in the two-millennia-old Christian tradition, placing himself far closer on the timeline of western art to Hieronymus Bosch than to Joseph Beuys.[23]

It's not only that Howson is understanding the world through a Christian framework – C.S. Lewis's 'true myth' – it also shapes his conception of his role as an artist. Describing his personal philosophy of art-making, he draws heavily on the Trinity Theory outlined by Dorothy L. Sayers in *The Mind of the Maker* (1941):

> For painting, it's like three circles ... The first circle is God, which is the idea; the second circle is Jesus Christ, which is the technique; and the third circle is the Holy Spirit, which is the message. You have to balance out these things in your painting ... If a painting or a piece of work doesn't convey a message ... it doesn't mean anything.[24]

Howson has said that this is 'the only way I understand what an artist is'.[25]

These ideas manifest in two distinct ways in his recent work, together making up the main force of his current practice. Both were present in his earlier work but have come to occupy a much more important position. One is the painting of single figures or small groups which focus on a single figure – usually a character from the Bible or a saint – which are characterised by stillness and psychological investigation. The second is the creation of complex compositions of multiple roiling bodies, often referencing hell, judgement or the apocalypse.

With regard to the first of these, a key example can be found in the story of one of Howson's most famous religious paintings. In 2008, he was commissioned by the Roman Catholic Church in Scotland to paint St John Ogilvie, martyred at Glasgow Cross in 1615 for preaching the Catholic faith when such preaching was outlawed, and canonised in 1976. At 8 x 3 metres, it was to be the largest crowd scene ever painted in Scotland and Howson's biggest work to date, and it was to hang in the newly refurbished Metropolitan Cathedral of St Andrew in Glasgow. A film crew making a BBC Scotland Artworks documentary would track its progress throughout.[26]

The project was beset by difficulties and delays. Howson said it took him to the edge of bankruptcy and of sanity.[27] When he finally began the painting, it was on a much smaller scale, but still featured a version of the crowd scene originally planned, a mob watching and jeering as the saint stood on the scaffold. After nine months' work, it was nearing completion when Howson, while the TV cameras rolled, grabbed a brush and began to cover it with black paint. He then started another painting which he completed much more quickly and presented to the Archdiocese.

The first one, he said, had been 'raw and cartoon-like'.[28] The second, which currently hangs in the cathedral,

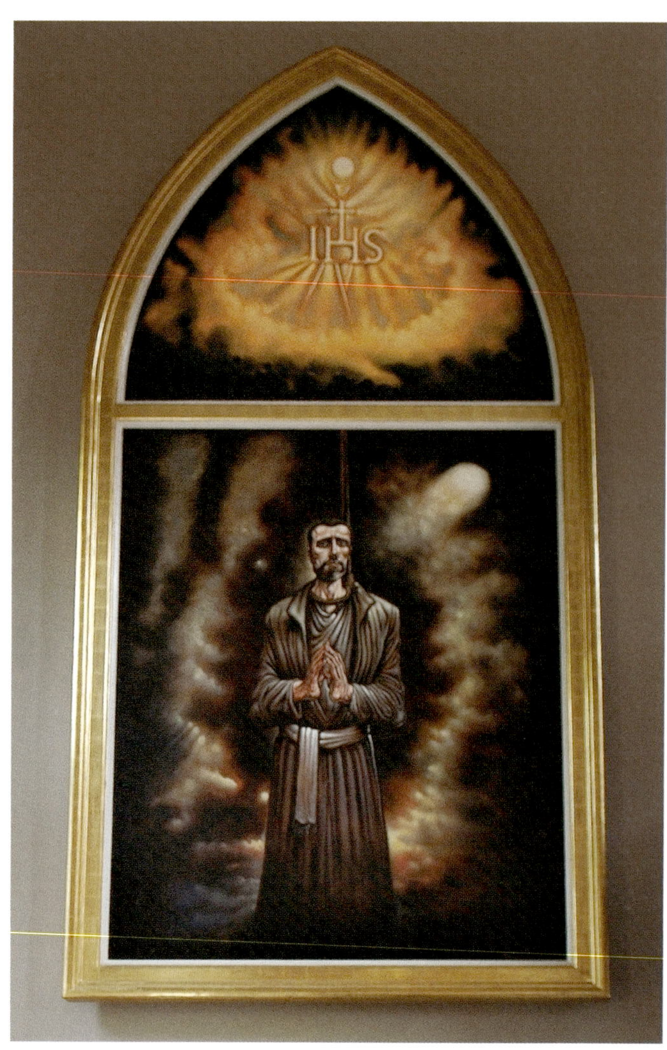

St John Ogilvie at St Andrew's Cathedral, Glasgow
2011 / oil on canvas
photograph Andy Buchanan / Alamy Stock Photo

is very different (2010/11, left). The crowd has disappeared, and Ogilvie appears elevated against a background of dark swirling cloud, as if he were already ascending into heaven. The noose is still around his neck, but it seems almost incidental. Howson had completed a large number of preparatory paintings and drawings exploring the possible expressions on the face of a man about to die for his faith,[29] and the final painting reads like the conclusion to these reflections. The light draws us to Ogilvie's face. His expression is calm and, while his hands are steepled in prayer, he looks not heavenward but directly at us, the crowd. His eyes are full of concern. I have worked out my salvation, he seems to say, what about you?

This change of direction also demonstrates what the best of Howson's religious painting is capable of: a subtle psychological exploration of an extraordinary experience. In *Job* (2011, p. 72), the subject is not alone, but the figures clustered round him are ancillary at best. Again, the light falls on his face, open and devoid of pretention; devoid of anger too, simply questioning the Almighty. *Road to Damascus* (2021, right) is unusual for a Howson painting in that the figure is not central, and only the face of the Apostle Paul is shown. At the centre of the picture is the light coming from the sky, the divine revelation. Paul's face is caught in that light, his eyes straying, his mouth half open; turned momentarily insensible by his experience. By contrast, in *St Francis* (2019, p. 18) the face of the saint is almost completely in shadow: the light falls on his nose and chin, his patched robe, his clasped hands, in which a skull is just visible. Again, it is a painting of a state of mind, a person transported by meditation, poised between life and death.

Something of the same detailed psychological examination comes through when Howson paints Jesus.

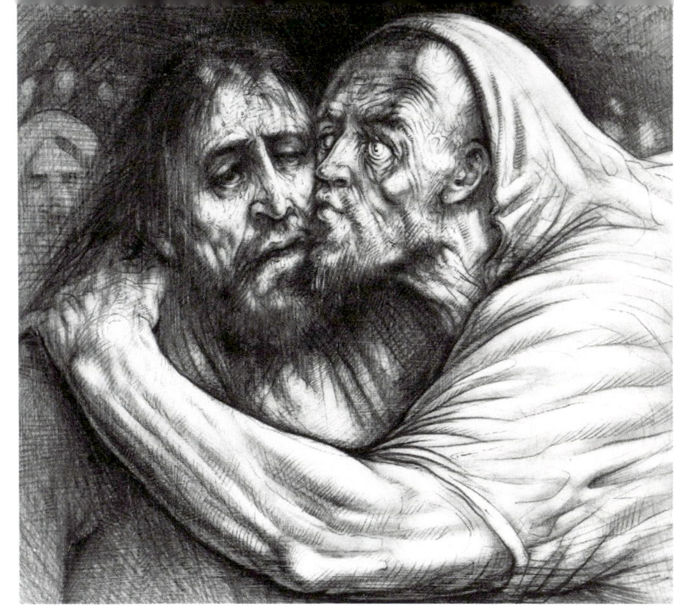

End of the Beginning
2008 / pencil on gessoed paper / 21.5 x 22.5 cm
private collection, Switzerland

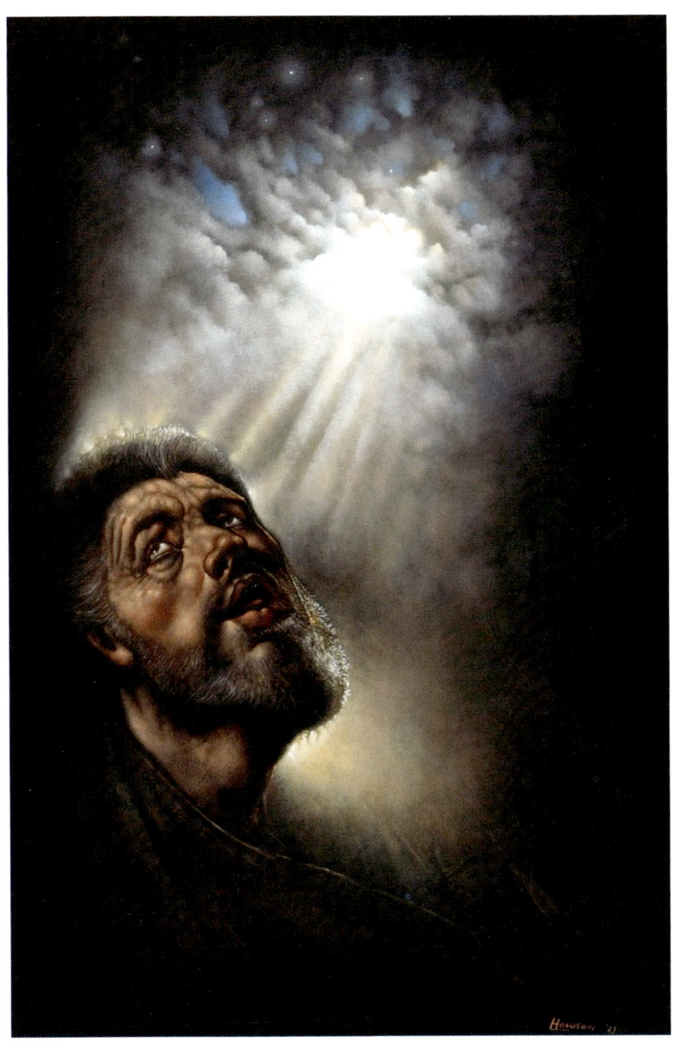

Road to Damascus
2021 / oil on gesso panel / 76 x 51 cm
John J. Studzinski CBE

He has been criticised for making Jesus too human, 'a victim not a redeemer'.[30] However, in mainstream Christian theology, Christ is both fully human and fully divine. Howson has simply chosen to emphasise his humanity. In *End of the Beginning* (2008, above), he draws the moment when Judas kisses Jesus to identify him to the Roman soldiers before his arrest. Jesus's face is weary with struggle, aged beyond his 33 years, not flinching from the embrace, but saddened by it. In his 'Stations of the Cross' series, the final paintings (such as *Jesus Is Taken Down from the Cross*, 2003, p. 63) have a strong focus on the face of Christ, running the gamut of emotions from resignation through weariness and anguish to death itself. Heller has described them as '14 close-ups of great and most painful beauty'.[31]

These quiet paintings, with their intense focus on psychological realism, sit in contrast to what I will call Howson's 'apocalyptic' paintings, in which a mass of figures seem to swirl in constant motion. These seethe with ideas and references as they do with bodies: aspects of Christian myth and tradition, Graeco-Roman myth, Dante's *Inferno*, Milton's *Paradise Lost*, William Blake, Hieronymus Bosch. In some, a crucified Christ is present; others are simply a tumult of distorted bodies, some grotesque, some monstrous. Caleb Froehlich describes the experience of looking at one such painting, *Prophecy* (2016, p. 76):

It is almost as if the mass is being continually reconstructed by various limbs and torsos through a seemingly endless piecing together, a perpetual reassembling ... Howson infuses order with chaos, and in so doing subverts what is natural or acceptable through overdose, an excess of the unnatural or the unacceptable. The mass assaults our vision,

preventing the viewer from identifying intelligible
human shapes.[32]

While the technical skills and compositional control needed to resolve these complex paintings is not in question,
the twenty-first-century viewer needs a context in which
to understand them. Writers have tended to focus on the
grotesque, contorted figures and conclude, as American
art critic David Cohen did, that Howson is 'surely happiest
in hell'.[33] But to read them simply as depictions of hell, or
of an imagined apocalypse, is not only to misunderstand
Howson's theology – it overlooks the other layers of
meaning in the work.

Howson has said that the paintings are not indicative
of his espousal of an arcane version of the Christian faith:
'I'm not a religious maniac that believes that some people
are saved and some people burn in hell.'[34] The imagery,
then, is at least partly metaphorical. It is worth noting
that Howson makes regular use of the imagery of hell to
describe certain life experiences. Bosnia was 'like being
in hell'. One psychiatric hospital stay was described in
hellish terms: 'Every night screaming, shouting, fighting,
arguing … like a nightmare, like bedlam.' The current
political situation in the UK is 'a kind of hell'. He com-
pares himself to Dante, whom, a friend of his once
wrote, was able to visit hell in his poetry, but came
back more damaged each time.[35]

In Charlie Paul's film, *Prophecy* (2019), which
followed the creation of the 2016 painting, Howson
explains his intentions:

> I think everyone with a mind would want to make
> sense of what's going on [in the world]. People
> don't realise how thin the veneer of civilisation
> is. Underneath is complete anarchy and chaos.

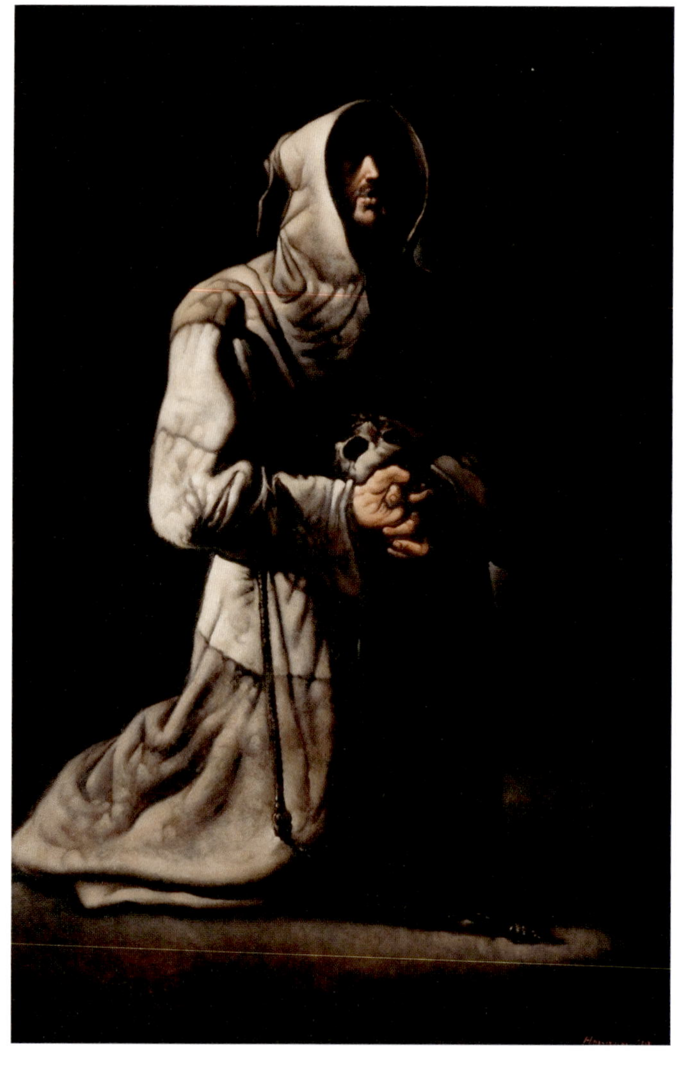

St Francis
2019 / oil on gesso panel / 75 x 50 cm
John J. Studzinski CBE

Just as, at Glasgow School of Art, he was encouraged by Sandy Moffat to make art which would comment on the state of the world, he is continuing to do so, using apocalyptic language.

Steven Berkoff has written that the work of artists like Howson follows 'a mythic route whereby we somehow recognise our world shockingly revealed'.[36] These paintings take their bearings, again, from Goya and Bosch, and from German Neue Sachlichkeit painters like Dix and Max Beckmann, painting what they saw as the moral bankruptcy of the Weimar Republic and the growing threat of Naziism. Ludwig Meidner, whose apocalyptic paintings of 1912 and 1913 prefigured the horrors of the First World War, is another touchstone. Jonathan Evens has written: 'Howson stands with all these artists, such as Bosch, Goya, Dix and Rouault, who have sought to raise our gaze from the mire by painting the extent to which we are sinking in the mire.'[37]

If the political and social critique in these paintings can be summarised, it might be as follows: a decadent society, focussed on materialism, is blind to the rise of dangerous ideas, and deaf to its responsibility towards the poor. However, different elements come to the surface in different works, with time periods and cultural references spliced and mingled. The rise of extremism continues to interest Howson. Some paintings feature flags – sometimes whole, sometimes in tatters: the Union Jack, the Stars and Stripes, the ISIS flag and now, also, the flag of Ukraine. Around the time of the Brexit vote, thugs wearing St George's Cross armbands began to appear. Often, there is an open sewer: a symbol of moral bankruptcy. During the Covid-19 pandemic,

facemasks and molecular depictions of the virus seamlessly joined the mix.

However hopeless all this might appear, Howson says his aim is 'to show people the reality of living in troubled times … to wake us all up, and give us hope'.[38] The presence of the crucified Christ in some of the paintings is a reminder that nothing is irredeemable. John A. Kohan writes that 'Christ's descent into hell after the crucifixion, known as "The Harrowing of Hell" … has become the defining narrative of Howson's life, faith and art.'[39] In his analysis of Howson's *Hades* paintings (as in *Hades IV*, 2011, p. 70), Caleb Froehlich describes how the figure of Christ descends to the different mythological levels of hell, mirroring what Christ finds there in his own body in order to bring salvation.[40] Froehlich adds that, for Howson, this is personal, too. In his darkest moments, he went to hell, and Christ was there with him.

Rowan Williams, former Archbishop of Canterbury, giving the Templeton Religion Trust Lecture at New College, University of Edinburgh in November 2022, described the deepest impulse in the creative act as one of reconciliation.[41] He went on to discuss what this could mean in relation to the work of Goya, who sought to depict war, injustice, violence and inhumanity, both real and imagined:

and compassion, and therefore that raw atrocity, unmitigated and unmediated pain, is not the fate of the world, not the last word or the defining word … In short, that kind of representation keeps alive the possibility of discovery, the possibility of breaking open in some way the ways in which we experience and receive the world, and so the possibility of hope and, dare we say, the possibility of grace within the workings of the world.

Howson's apocalyptic paintings don't often depict grace. There is energy in the swirling, grotesque darkness. He admits that, when he looks at Gustave Doré's illustrations for *Paradise Lost*, he finds the pictures of heaven 'boring'. There is vitality in hell and, fifty years on from his very early apocalyptic drawings, the apocalypse is still exciting: *What Can't be Cured Must be Endured* (2021, p. 97). But he is searching in that darkness for light, for truth. He describes finding that same search on the faces of alcoholics, 'down-and-outs' and the people he has met at AA meetings:

The whole thing is the search for truth. They're going about it the wrong way with the drink and the drugs, but they're still searching. It's much better to be like that, to search, even if you fail, than live the suburban life where you're always looking at your neighbours, what kind of car they've got … If there's no such thing as truth, why are we here?

Returning to the studio after one of his periods in hospital, Howson describes how he listened obsessively to the audio book of C.S. Lewis's *The Pilgrim's Regress*. Written within a year of the author's own conversion to Christianity, it is a kind of Pilgrim's

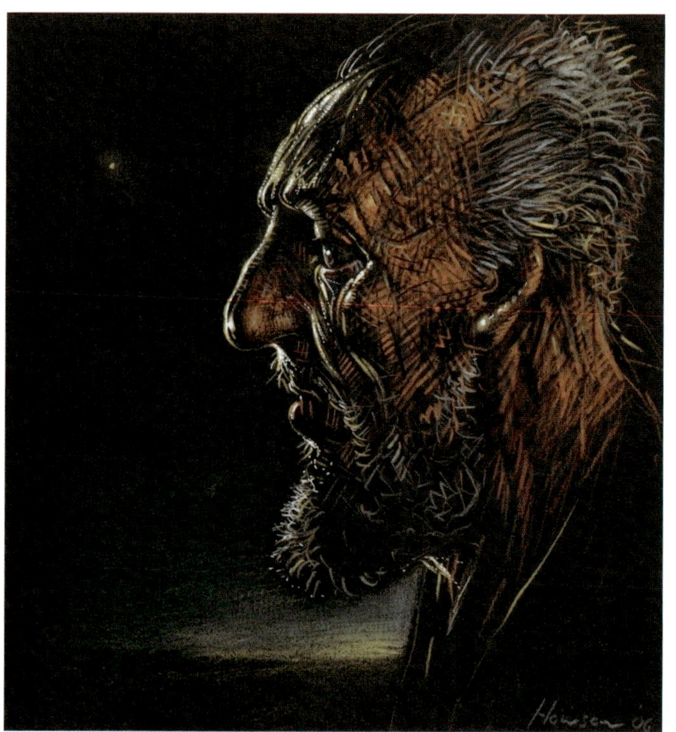

Andrew
2006 / pastel on paper / 21 x 20 cm
City Art Centre, Edinburgh Museums and Galleries
photograph Antonia Reeve

Progress for the early twentieth century – a search narrative in which the pilgrim, John, pursues what he longs for, gradually unmasking one false desire after another until only one remains: the desire for God.

Nearing the end of his journey, John looks back on the road he has travelled, expecting to see the landscapes he remembers:

> But there was nothing of the kind: only the long straight road, very narrow, and on the left crags, rising within a few paces of the road into ice and mist and, beyond that, black cloud; on the right, swamps and jungle sinking almost at once into black cloud.[42]

It is a path between heaven and hell. Lewis sums it up in one of his final poems in the book:

> All that seemed earth is Hell, or Heaven.
> God is: thou art:
> The rest, illusion.[32]

Howson, in his mid-sixties at the time of writing, has some of that clarity of vision. He is wiser, chastened; he no longer brags about recovery, says only that life is stable, as stable as it has been for some time. He is sustained by his partner, Lorraine, his daughter Lucie, and his work. For an artist, the search for truth is about becoming a better artist. He speaks about wanting to be as good as Dürer or Goya, about wanting to paint a picture worthy of Bellini's *St Francis in the Desert*. He wonders if he has enough time. For this reason, he walks the path along the precipice daily. The path that leads to the studio.

1. Robert Heller, *Peter Howson* (Momentum, 2003), p. 41.
2. Ibid., p. 44.
3. Ibid., p. 75.
4. Alan Jackson, *A Different Man: Peter Howson's Art from Bosnia and Beyond* (Mainstream, 1997), p. 22.
5. Ibid., p. 70.
6. Ibid., p. 70.
7. Robert Crampton, 'Facing Fear: Peter Howson in Bosnia', *Peter Howson: Bosnia* (Imperial War Museum, 1994), p. 14.
8. Ibid., p. 11.
9. Jackson, p. 102.
10. Ibid., p. 109.
11. Ibid., p. 112.
12. Heller, p. 150.
13. Emily Spicer, 'Peter Howson Interview', *Studio International*, 2013, www.studiointernational.com.
14. Kay Redfield Jamison, *Touched with Fire: Manic Depressive Illness and the Artistic Temperament* (Simon & Schuster, 1993), p. 5.
15. Ibid., p. 76.
16. Ibid., p. 2.
17. Ibid., p. 54.
18. Ibid., p. 54.
19. Ibid., p. 122.
20. Ibid., p. 122.
21. Jackson, p. 112.
22. Caleb Froehlich, 'Peter Howson and the Language of Salvation: The Role of the Grotesque in Redemption's Hades Cycle', *Religion and the Arts*, vol. 23, no. 1–2 (2019), pp. 76–99.
23. John A. Kohan, 'Peter Howson and the Harrowing of Hell', *Image Journal*, no. 76, www.imagejournal.org.
24. Spicer.
25. Jonathan Evens, *Peter Howson Artlyst Interview*, 26 November 2018, www.artlyst.com.
26. 'The Madness of Peter Howson', BBC Scotland, Artworks, 2010.
27. Ibid.
28. Ibid.
29. *Peter Howson: Saint John Ogilvie* (Archdiocese of Glasgow, 2011).
30. Donald Kuspit, 'Bipolar Paintings – Peter Howson: The Scottish Bosch', *Artnet Magazine*, 29 March 2012, www.artnet.com.
31. Heller, p. 227.
32. Froehlich.
33. David Cohen, 'Hell and Back: The Religious Paintings of Peter Howson', *Art Critical*, 3 May 2012, www.artcritical.com.
34. Spicer.
35. Susan Mansfield, 'Artist Peter Howson Returns after Depression Battle', *The Scotsman*, 2 March 2013.
36. Steven Berkoff, 'Introduction', *Acheron and Other Works/Christos Aneste/Stations of the Cross* (Flowers Gallery, 2005), p. 3.
37. Jonathan Evens, 'Peter Howson: The Play Is Over – Flowers Gallery', *Artlyst*, 10 November 2018, www.artlyst.com.
38. Ibid.
39. Kohan.
40. Froehlich.
41. Rowan Williams, 'Seeing the Light: Epiphany in the Visual Arts', New College, Edinburgh, 5 November 2022.
42. C.S. Lewis, *The Pilgrim's Regress* (Fount/Harper Collins, 1933; this edition 1998), p. 221.
43. Ibid., p. 222.

THE BOXER

Matthew Flowers

In 1985 the seminal exhibition *New Image Glasgow* opened at the Third Eye Centre in Glasgow. It travelled through the United Kingdom, and as part of this tour arrived at the Air Gallery, London. A compelling review of the exhibition by Waldemar Januszczak in *The Guardian* took me almost immediately to see the show, which included four painters who were dubbed 'The New Glasgow Boys' – Steven Campbell, Adrian Wiszniewski, Peter Howson and Ken Currie – as well as Stephen Barclay and Mario Rossi. While every artist was strong and had something meaningful to relay, Peter Howson's work stood out for me. One of his *New Image* paintings that stopped me in my tracks was *The Boxer* (1985, right).

A towering 2 x 1.5 metre canvas depicting a rugged, statuesque man, one enormous leg in front of the other with his bare fists held up in front of his body, the boxer was wearing a stretched t-shirt showing bulging, over-sized muscles. The painting seemed sculptural and even animated, all-encompassing in its energy, towering over me. Its power and scale were overwhelming, and I understood immediately that I had come across a painter with whom I wanted to work.

After tracking Peter down and making a quick dash to Glasgow from London, I soon realised he had attracted the attention of other commercial art dealers. I worked with one of our directors, the late journalist Robert Heller, to place a small but significant feature on Peter in *The Telegraph* and then arranged for my mother and the gallery's founder, Angela Flowers, to invite Peter for tea at the Ritz in London. Looking every bit the part of an artist who had come straight from a paint-splattered studio, Peter turned up dressed down with no tie, so they were refused entry and ended up at a local café, where they got on like a house on fire. With an alignment of

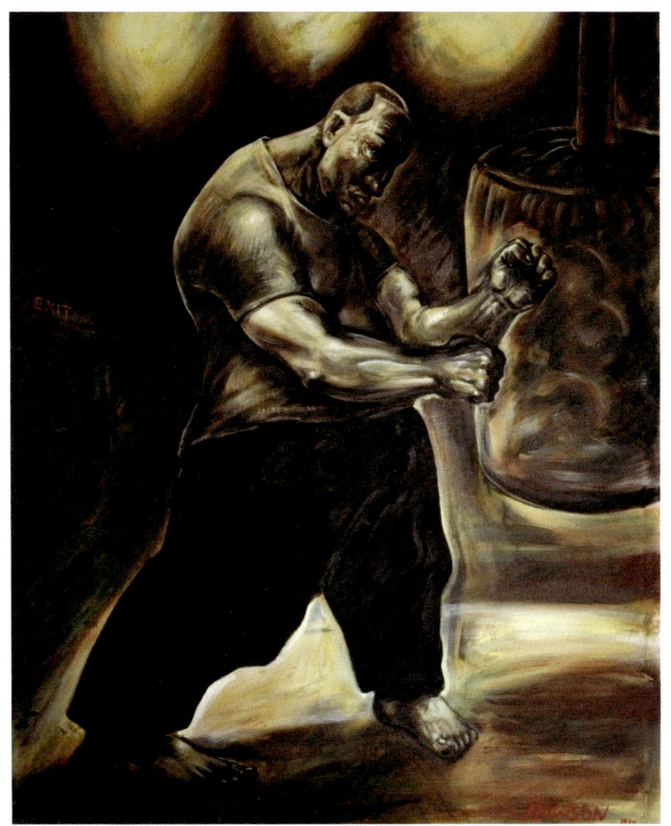

The Boxer
1985 / oil on canvas / 183 x 152 cm
private collection / photograph Ian Marshall

visions for his career and a natural chemistry between us all, we managed to persuade Peter that we were the right people to work with and a journey, now spanning almost forty years, ensued.

Peter and I have become close friends over the decades. Our relationship was cemented by riding a fast momentum of exhibitions and interest from collectors and institutions in the early days. At very short notice, in January 1987 we staged an introductory exhibition of a few of his paintings in our gallery at Tottenham Mews, London, with Howson in the gallery's second space and the abstractionist Terry Frost in our main space upstairs. Everything of Peter's sold – and to some very important collections. A few months later our gallery participated in the international art fair in Chicago. We decided to go all in and exhibit a huge newly finished painting, *The Heroic Dosser* (1987, p. 11) in the middle of our booth. It was purchased on the opening night by a major US collector. Two months later Peter's work was included in the *Vigorous Imagination* exhibition at the Scottish National Gallery of Modern Art in Edinburgh, curated by the art critic Clare Henry and Keith Hartley, curator at the SNGMA. They were keen to include the dynamic *Heroic Dosser* and shipped it over from America specially. The collector was so honoured that he donated the painting to the collection – the gallery's second Howson acquisition that year.

This was followed in 1987 with a solo exhibition in our main London gallery space, with a catalogue written by Januszczak. To prepare the catalogue text it was decided that Waldemar and I should visit Glasgow to view at first hand some of Peter's haunts, including the infamous Saracen Head pub, whose re-visioned inhabitants would feature in his set of 25 extraordinary etchings (1988, right, pp. 34–35). Peter's studio was in

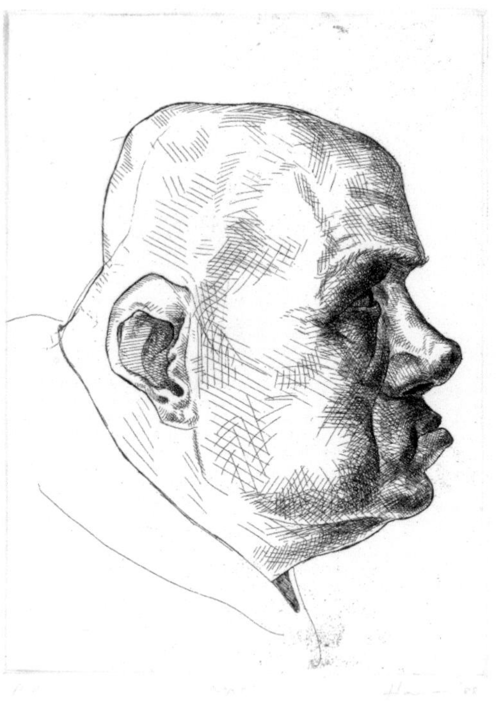

Saracen Heads: Mac
1988 / etching on paper / 56 x 38 cm
edition of 30 / published by Flowers Gallery / photograph Antonio Parente

the tough East End of the city, his studio complex buzzing with extraordinarily talented artists. Ken Currie was close by, and Peter invited him to join us on the local tour. As we took in the community and streets that inspired Peter's body of work, it was inevitable that, back in London, the exhibition was a smash success.

To round the year off, a new collector of Peter's, music promoter Gary Kurfirst, invited Peter to his home in Los Angeles. Peter didn't like the idea of travelling alone so we decided to go together, which began the development of a significant body of US collectors, initially many of whom were in the music industry.

Peter was included in American museum exhibitions including *The New British Painting*, which began at Cincinnati's Contemporary Arts Center and toured to other institutions in the USA. At the same time, he was winning over a following of American collectors such as Robert and Susan Kasen Summer, who became incredible friends to Peter over the years. He got a taste for travelling and the late '80s nightclub scene in New York, fuelling more material for paintings including *The Three Faces of Eve* (1990), a triptych featuring the midtown Au Bar nightclub in the middle panel (right). This was shown in a three-person exhibition with John Bellany and Jock McFadyen at the Pamela Auchincloss Gallery in New York.

These early years of fast success and endless travel took a toll on Peter. His focus momentarily stalled until a significant commission was offered to him by London's Imperial War Museum in 1993, proposing Peter as the official war artist to cover the Bosnian conflict. At the time the museum was short of funding but managed to get sponsorship from *The Times*. It was a real coup for Peter, and he took to the commission with drive and relish, leading to four major features in *The Times* Saturday magazine.

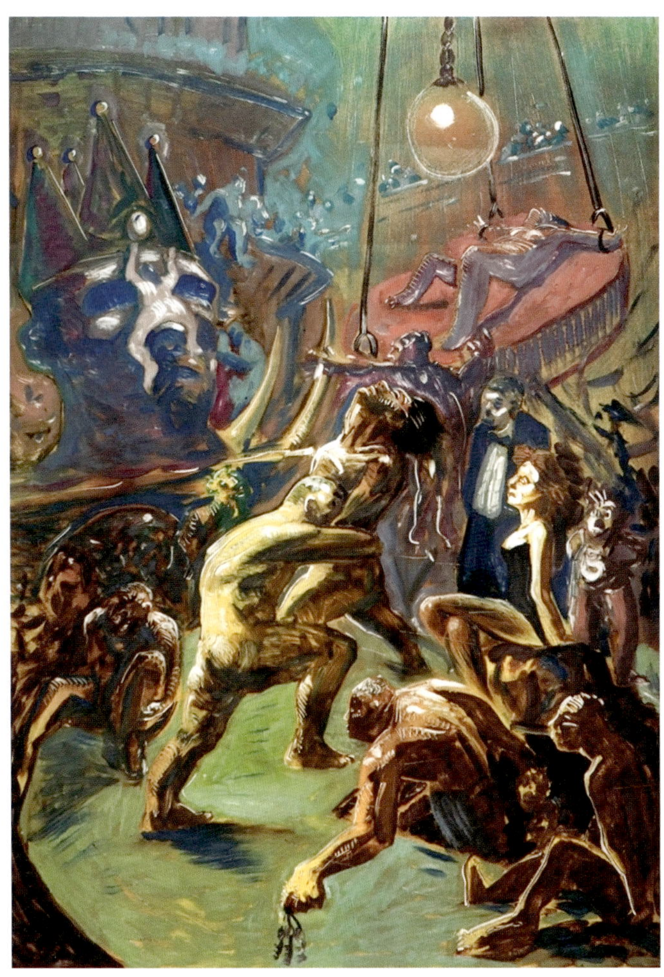

Au Bar II
1990 / monoprint on paper / 133 x 81cm
Flowers Gallery / photograph Antonio Parente

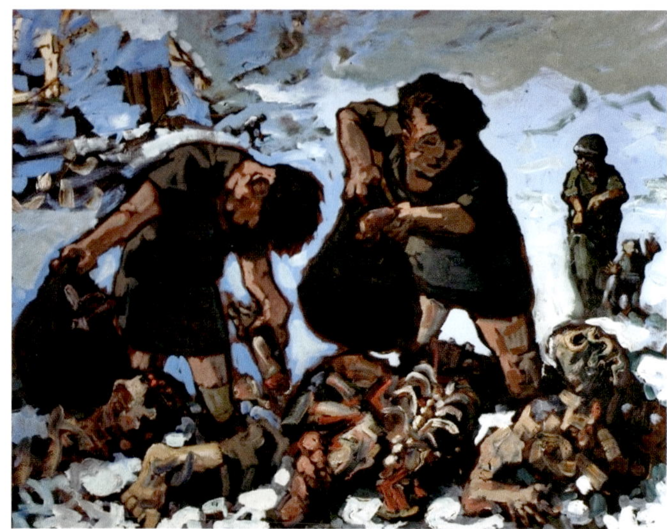

Bosnian Harvest
1994 / oil on canvas / 122.5 x 142.5 cm
Nottingham City Museums and Galleries

Peter came to stay with me ahead of his departure to Bosnia and I drove him to RAF Brize Norton, Oxfordshire, the night before his departure. Despite the reports coming from the area, neither of us had any idea of the true scope of horrors that he would face, and how that would affect him. It was an overwhelming experience across the board, and he left Bosnia earlier than planned due to dysentery, unable to work in full. His experience there was recorded, scrutinised and aired on TV by a trailing crew from the BBC, and on his return to Glasgow he was greeted with a hurtful backlash in the media for not staying in the war zone longer.

A few months later, a second trip gave him the material he needed to produce a prolific body of work – paintings, drawings, prints – fresh, raw and very much depicting the rage and helplessness he felt as an outsider (such as *Bosnian Harvest*, 1994, above). He listened to harrowing stories of refugees that he got involved with helping, depicting the cruel atrocities described to him in a difficult body of work. The ensuing exhibitions at the Imperial War Museum and our gallery in the East End of London were highly acclaimed, leading to museum acquisitions of the work. This was followed by introductions to and relationships with major inter-national collectors including David Bowie, who bought the infamous *Bosnian Rape* painting that the Imperial War Museum controversially refused to buy despite their chief curator campaigning for it.

The experience of being in a violent war zone, and a lack of support in processing it, was traumatic for Peter. His mental health and personal life suffered, and it was difficult for any of his family and friends, including me, to know what to do. The displaced refugees' accounts that he was confronted with in Bosnia – including beheadings, rape and child abuse – haunted him, and

the press were on his back. His family life suffered and, sadly, he split up with his wife Terry.

This was incredibly painful for Peter, who doted on his autistic daughter Lucie. He struggled enormously with the estrangement, and I did my best to support him, not really knowing how to help him navigate the grief and trauma of being in a war zone, and the complicated guilt that came with being a reporter on the peripheries of conflict. I muddled through, and being there for him during this period brought us closer together.

Peter moved down to London to paint most of the Bosnian works. I found him studios to work in and a small house next door to me to live in, which gave us the opportunity to see more of each other, to have small daily interactions that focussed on the grounding routines of everyday life. London provided him with a certain healing space, and naturally became its own source of material.

Projects outside of the Bosnia work were a welcome relief, including a commission by Scottish Opera to create stage sets and costumes for a 1995 production of Mozart's *Don Giovanni*, a painting for Channel 4's TV series *Inside Art*, and a painting commissioned by TV scriptwriter Dean Lemmon, who was suffering from AIDS and knew he didn't have long to live. Peter made an extraordinary image of Dean that held no punches. We were able to include it in a 1996 group exhibition titled *Naked*, where it hung alongside Lucian Freud's *Benefits Supervisor Resting* (1994). A 1995 series of paintings making up 'The Rake's Progress' and based on Stravinsky's opera was significant – Peter identified very closely with the rake and in the series of seven paintings (p. 14) clearly depicted himself as the protagonist ending up in the mental asylum. I saw a reflection of Peter's internal struggles in all of these projects, and could usually

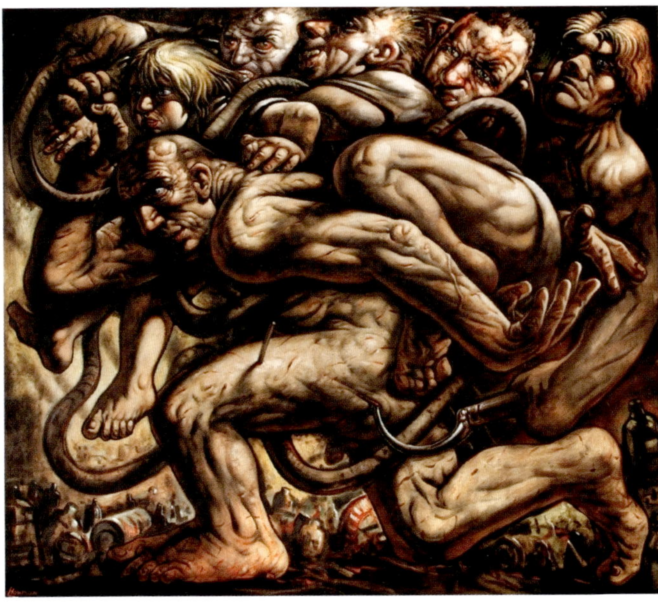

The First Step
2000 / oil on canvas / 180 x 214 cm
private collection

identify an image of him within the paintings themselves. It was not unusual to find this quality in much of his work, and it is also evident in the 'Underground' series, an incredible suite of delicate yet hard etchings made in the late '90s and depicting a portrait named after each London Underground station. Despite the portraits being anonymous male and female figures, to me Peter himself often emerges as both the artist and the subject.

As the '90s progressed Peter returned to Glasgow, and many of the dark sides of his life resurfaced, including substance misuse. Bravely, he entered a 12-step programme, embracing the opportunity to get himself through difficulties. During this period he produced some memorable work – particularly *The First Step* (2000, left), a painting that appears on the cover of the most important monograph to date, which Peter and I worked on in 2003. It was also a period in which remarkable sacred work started to appear. Always a man of faith, an early sign of these works could be seen in *Man of Sorrows* from 1998, but the deeply moving 'Stations of the Cross' series from 2003 brought divinity to prominence along with yet another significant audience for Peter's work. I saw clearly how Peter humbly reached for faith as support and guidance, and the relevant pictures reflect hope in the midst of chaos. A film of Peter creating a large religious crowd painting was commissioned by the BBC in 2009. It showed just how hard life had become for him. 'The Madness of Peter Howson' was released by the BBC in 2010.

The last twenty years have seen equal measures of turbulence and calm, but Peter made two incredibly important partnerships. One with Lorraine, who has brought love, support and humour into Peter's life, and the other with Stan, who has steered Peter to a stable and well-managed life. Peter continues to make some of the most compelling art for the times we live in.

A more positive film, *Prophecy*, which gives great insights into an artist's working practice, was released in 2019. It tracks the conception, production, exhibition and acquisition of an eponymous monumental painting (p. 76), showing Peter at his most vulnerable and inspired. The ink drawings started at the outset of the Covid pandemic are miraculous, Bosch-like masterpieces (including *What Can't Be Cured Must Be Endured*, 2021, p. 97). Together with the recent large-scale apocalyptic paintings they take on many of the tough global themes facing the world today, resonating with uncertainty, faith and power.

I am extremely proud to have worked with Peter for almost forty years, and even prouder to call him a friend.

ARTWORKS

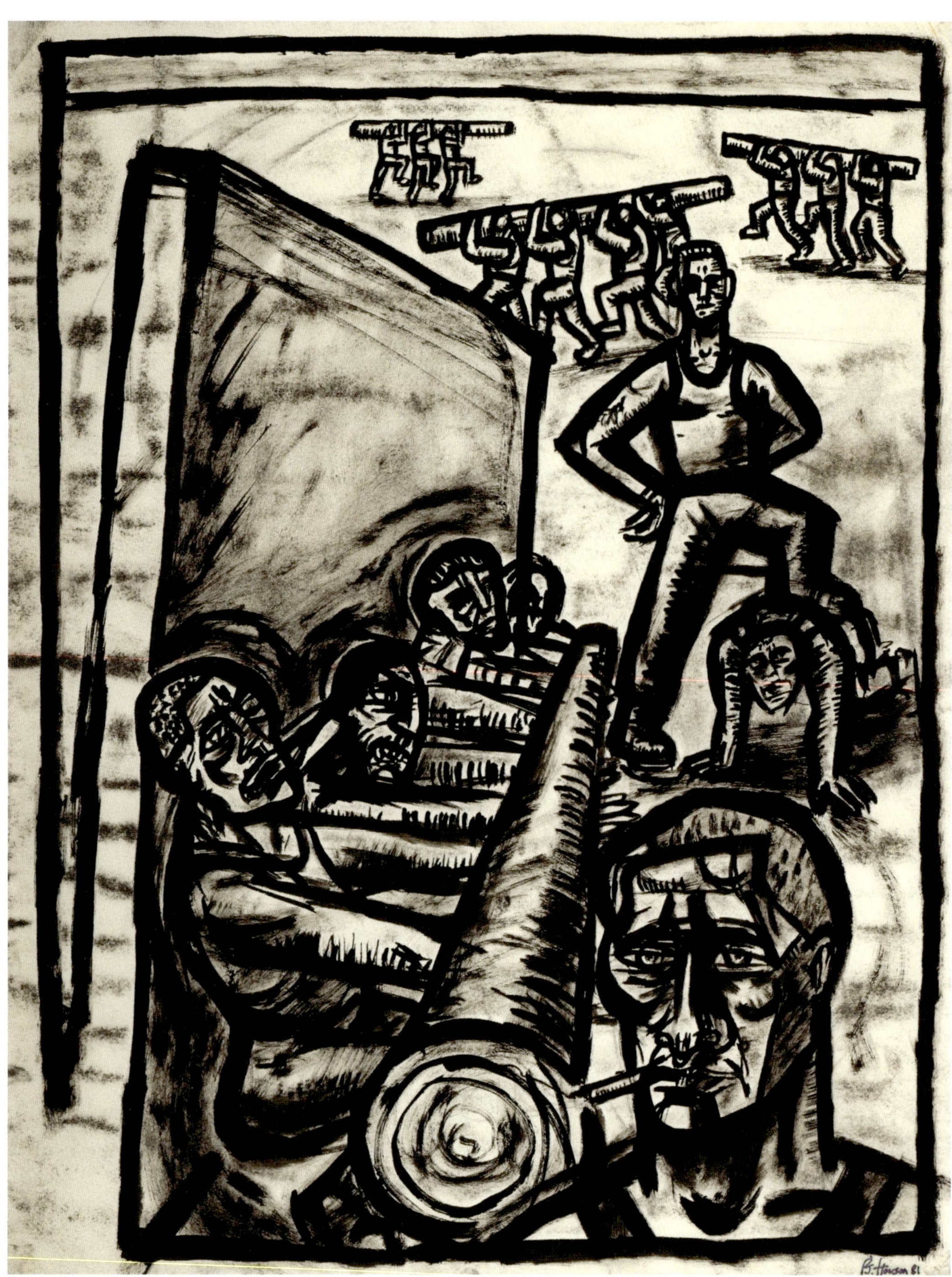

Exercise Yard
1981 / ink and charcoal on paper / 57 x 44.5 cm
Alexander Moffat / photograph Antonia Reeve

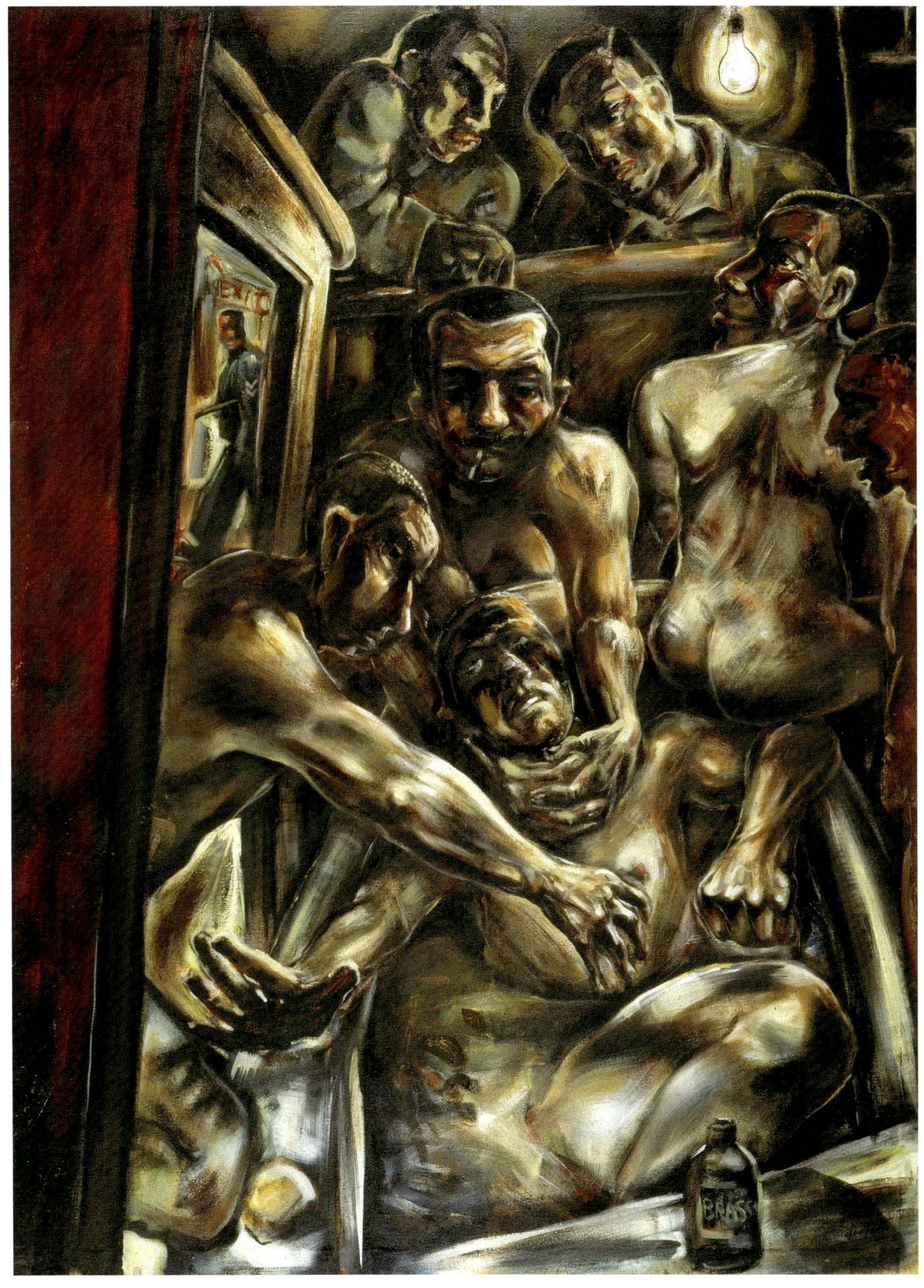

Regimental Bath
1985 / oil on canvas / 185 x 138 cm
City Art Centre, Edinburgh Museums and Galleries

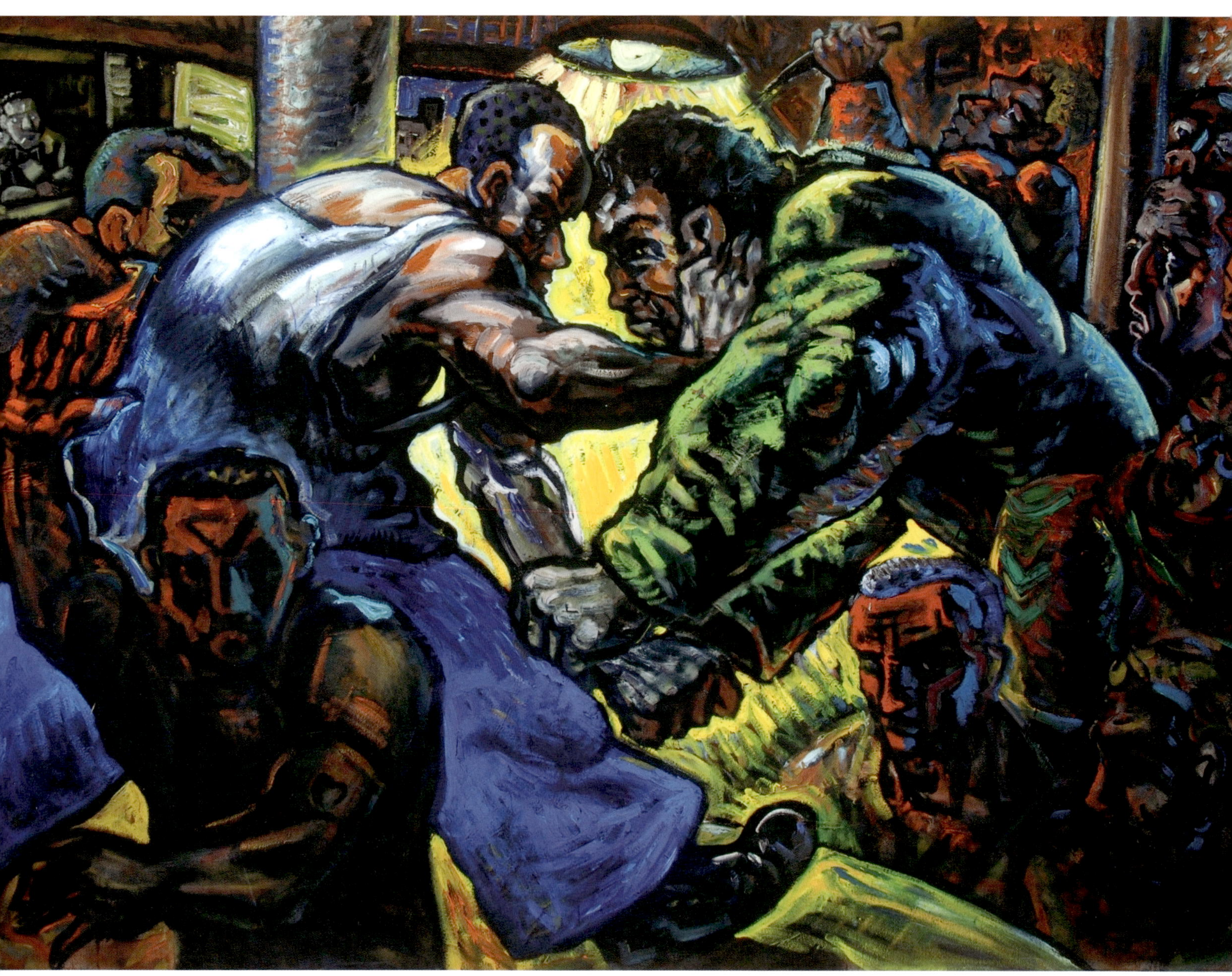

Saturday Night at Glencorse
1985 / oil on canvas / 187 x 258 cm
Middlesbrough Institute of Modern Art, MIMA

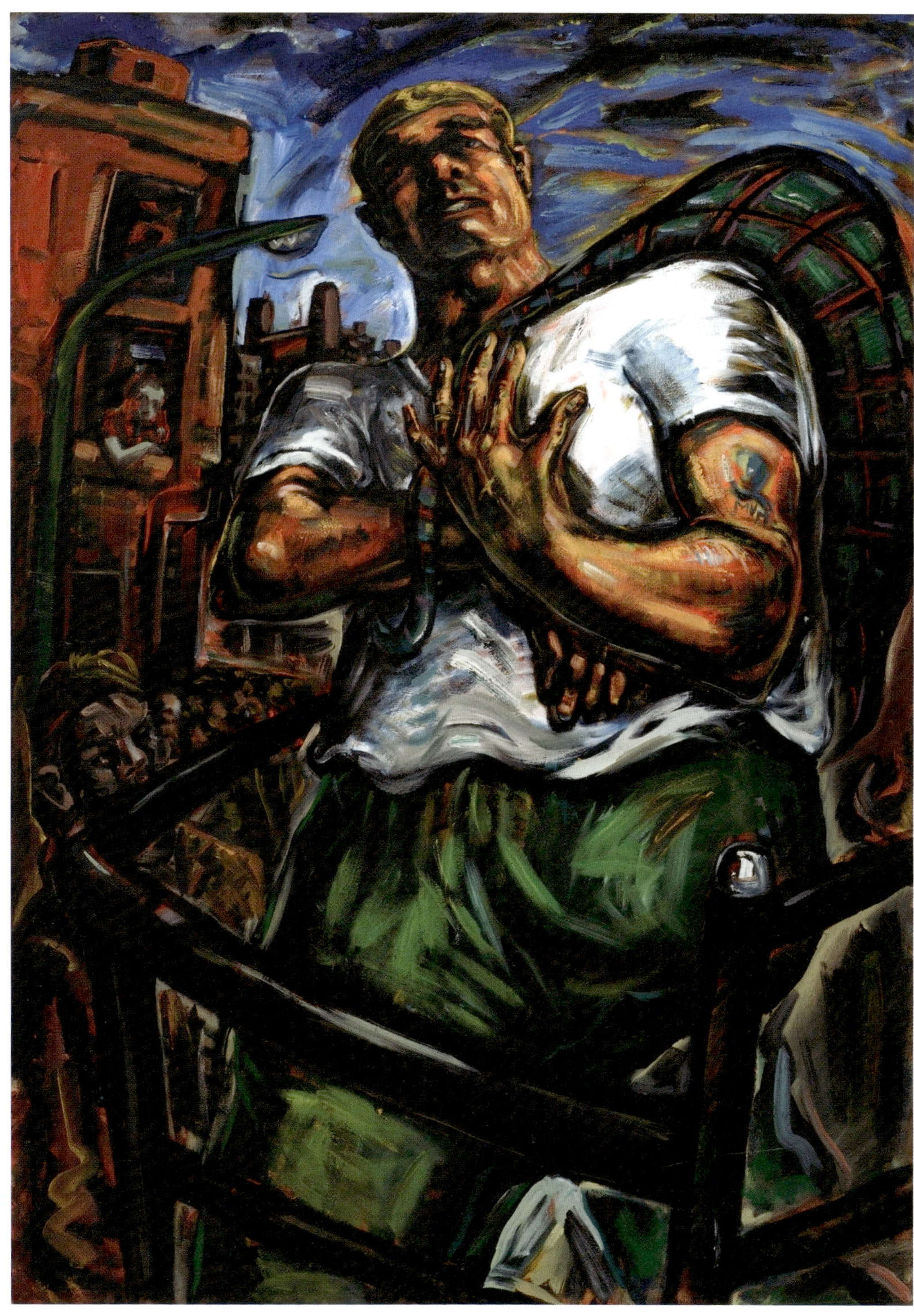

Lowland Hero Spurns the Cynic
1985 / oil on canvas / 214 x 153 cm
High Life Highland, Inverness Museum and Art Gallery

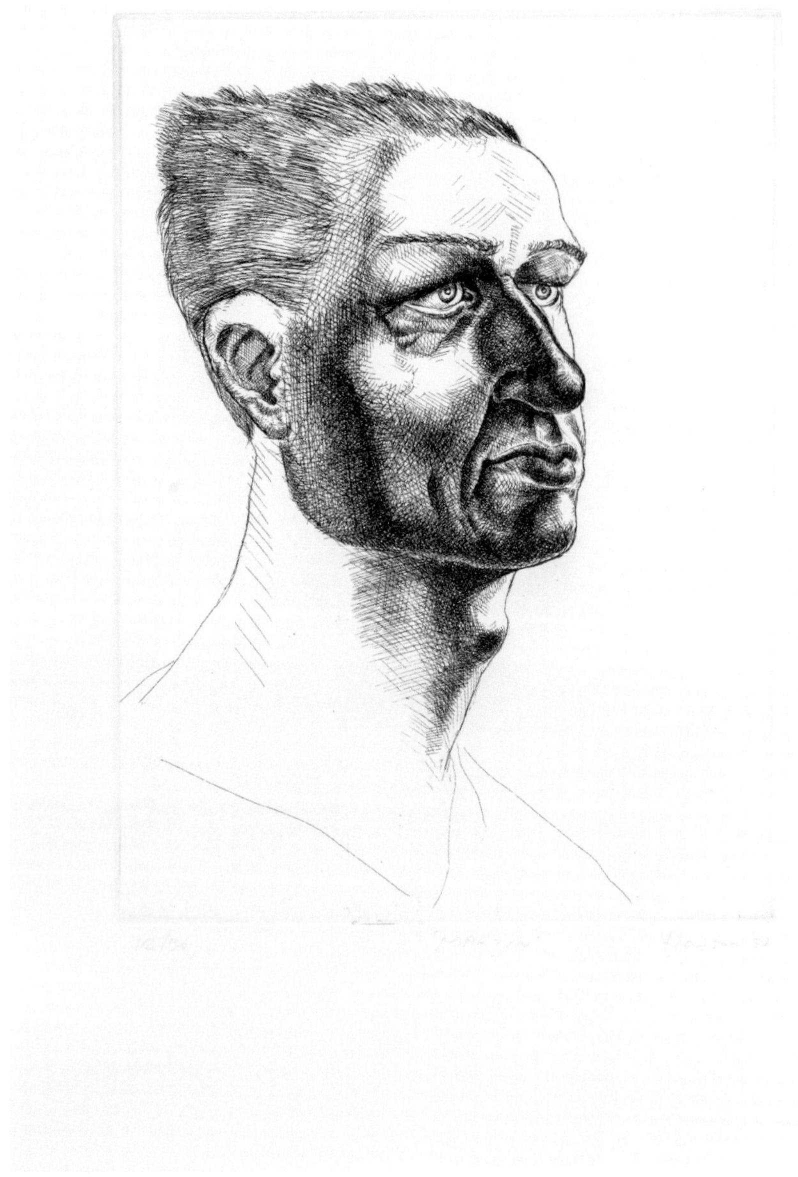

Saracen Heads
Martin
1988 / etching on paper / 56 x 38 cm
edition of 30 / published by Flowers Gallery / photograph Antonio Parente

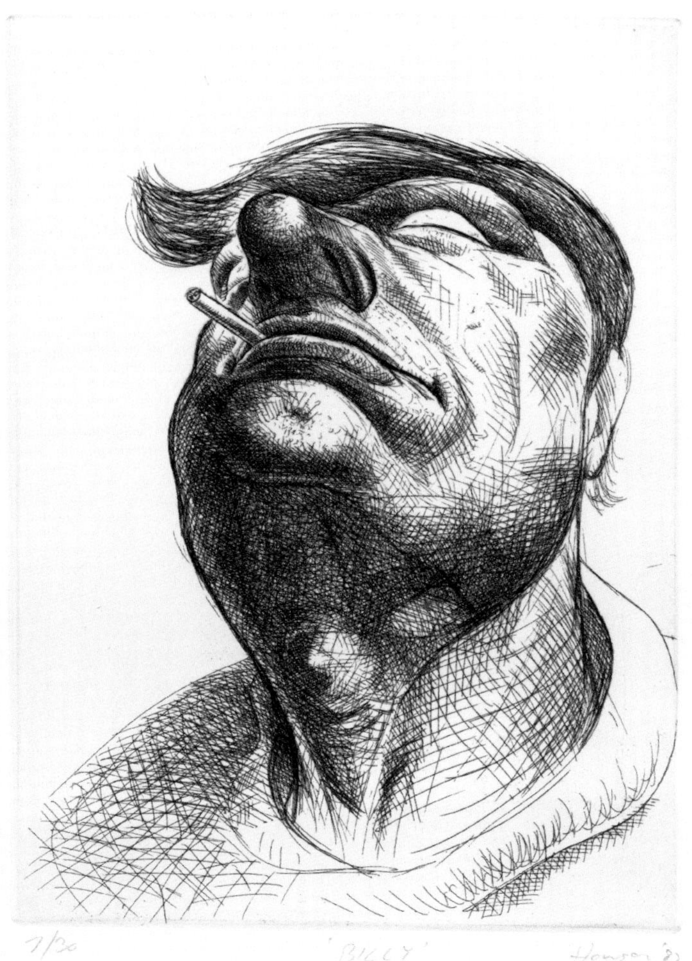

Saracen Heads
Billy
1988 / etching on paper / 56 x 38 cm
edition of 30 / published by Flowers Gallery / photograph Antonio Parente

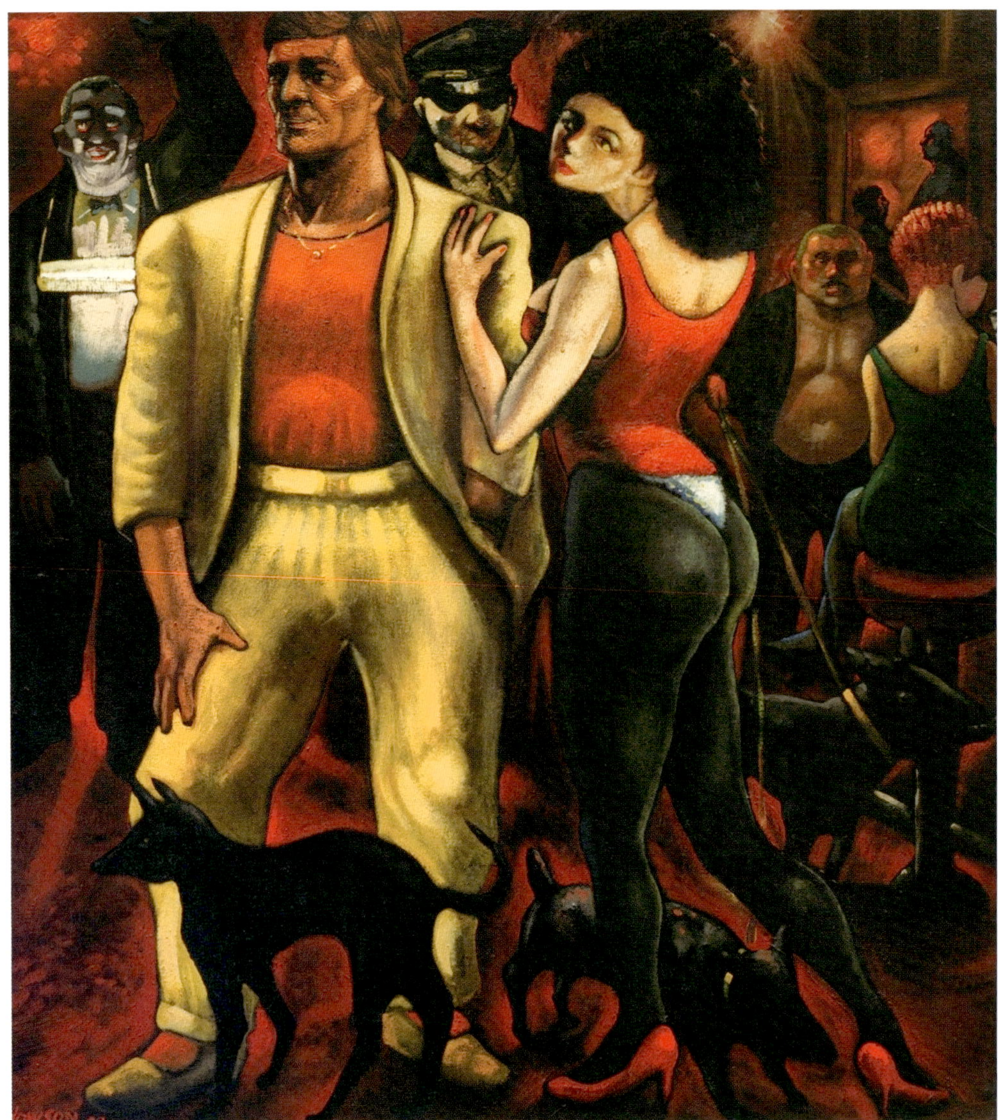

Limelight
1989 / oil on canvas / 110 x 101.5 cm
private collection / photograph Ian Marshall

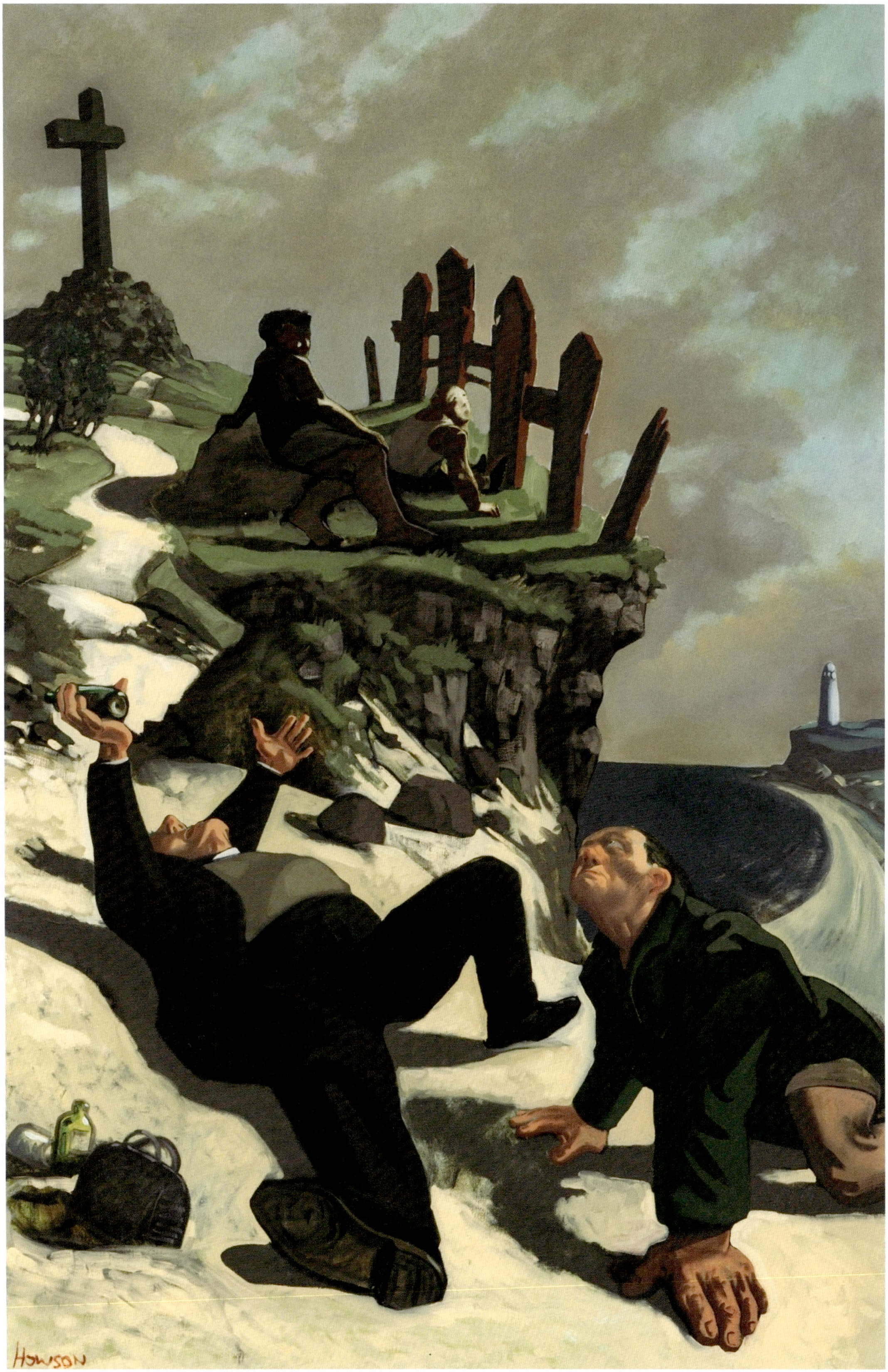

Wages of Sin
1990 / oil on canvas / 183 x 122 cm
private collection / photograph Antonio Parente

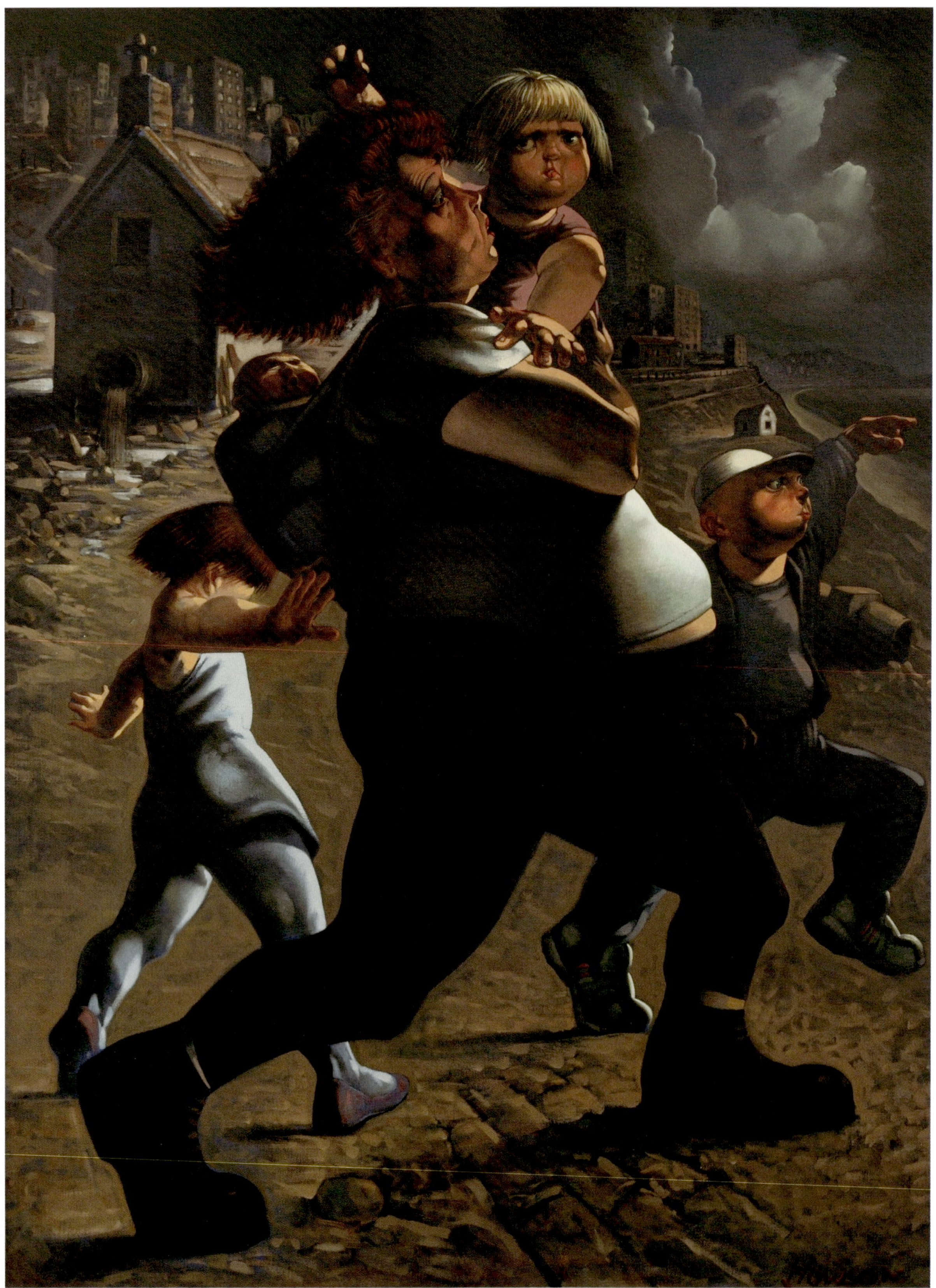

Blind Leading the Blind I (Mother & Daughter)
1991 / oil on canvas / 244 x 183 cm
private collection / photograph Antonio Parente

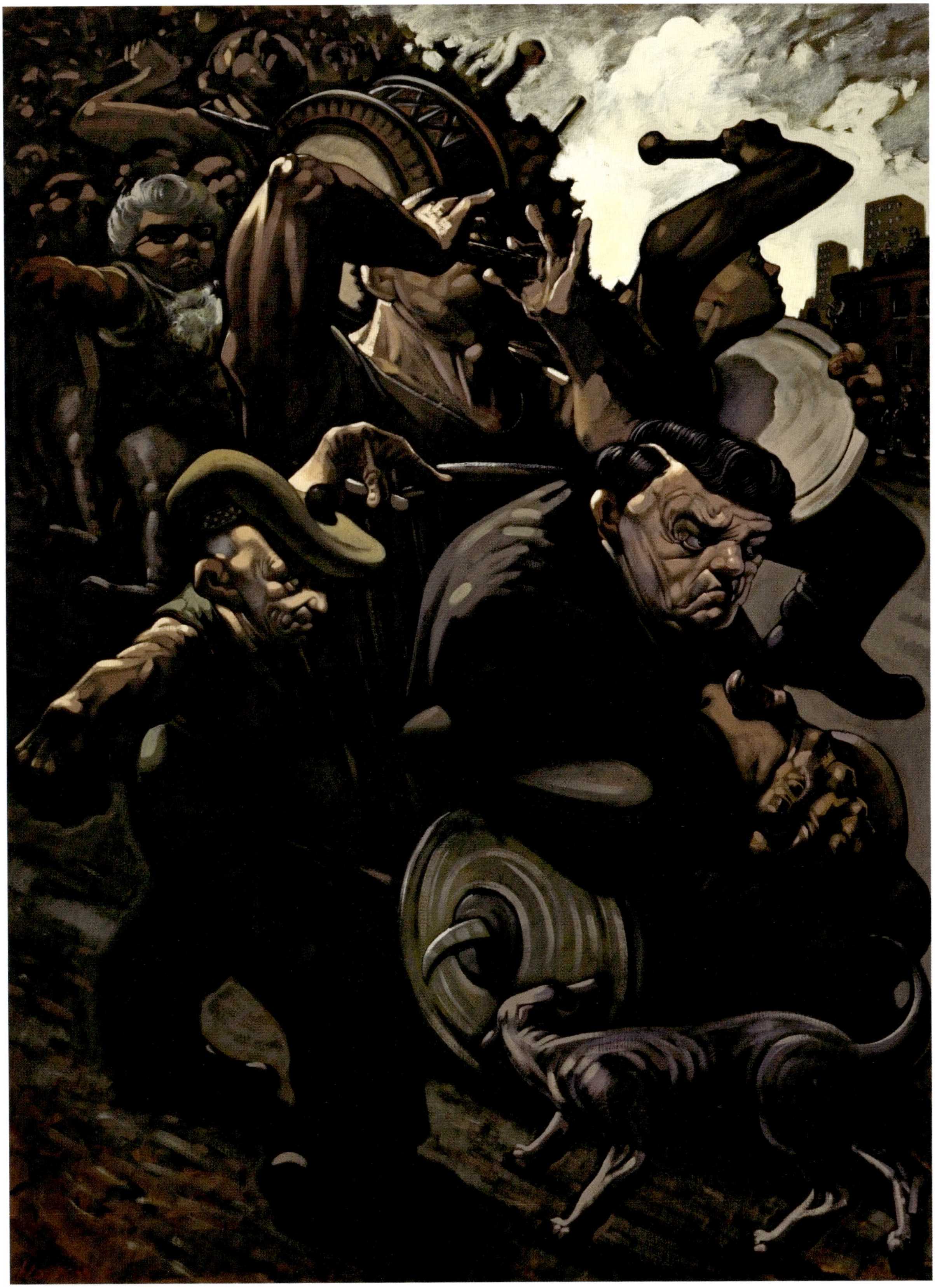

Blind Leading the Blind III (Orange Parade)
1991 / oil on canvas / 244 x 183 cm
private collection / photograph Antonio Parente

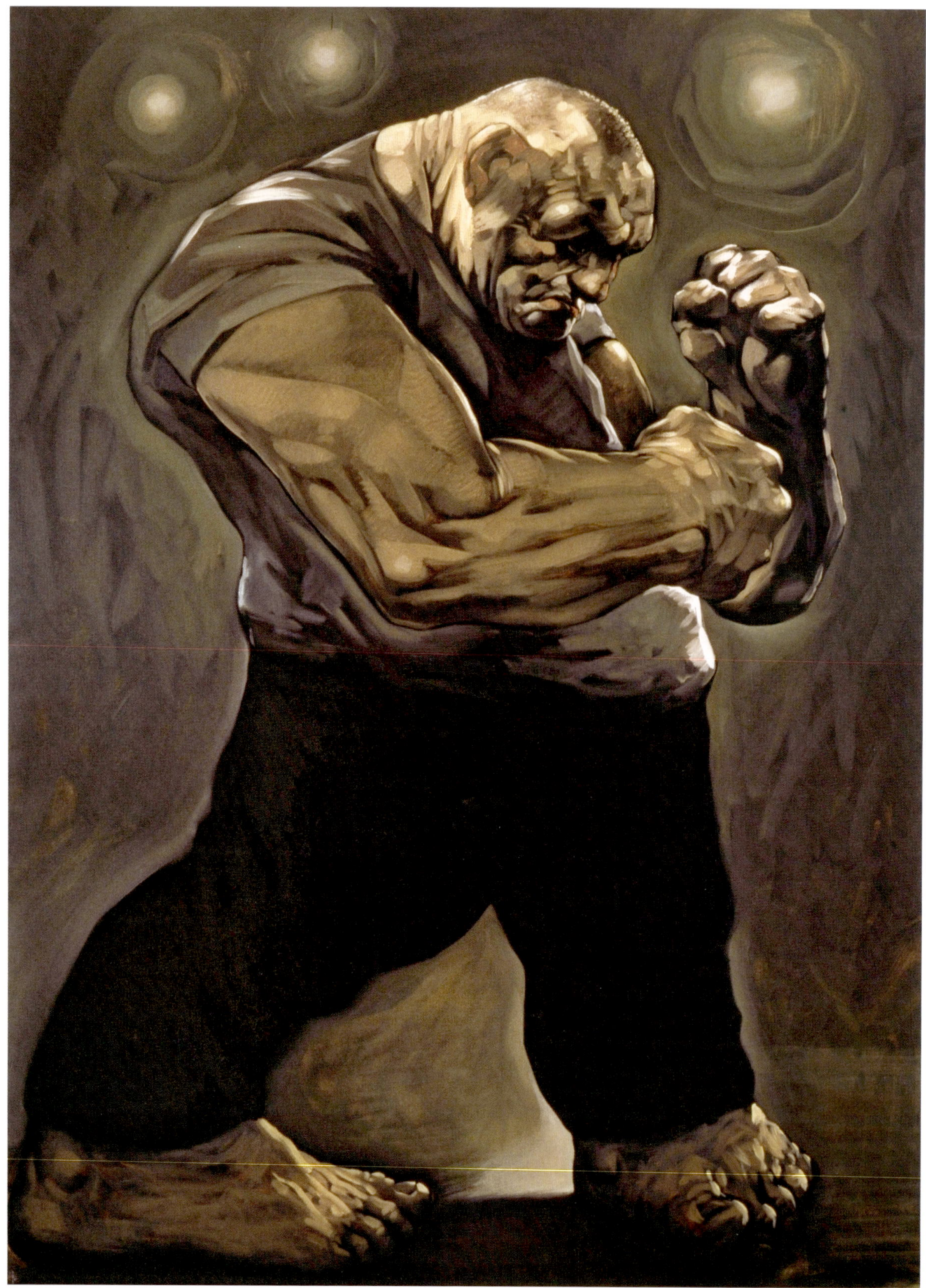

Blind Leading the Blind VI (Boxer)
1991 / oil on canvas / 244 x 183 cm
private collection / photograph Antonio Parente

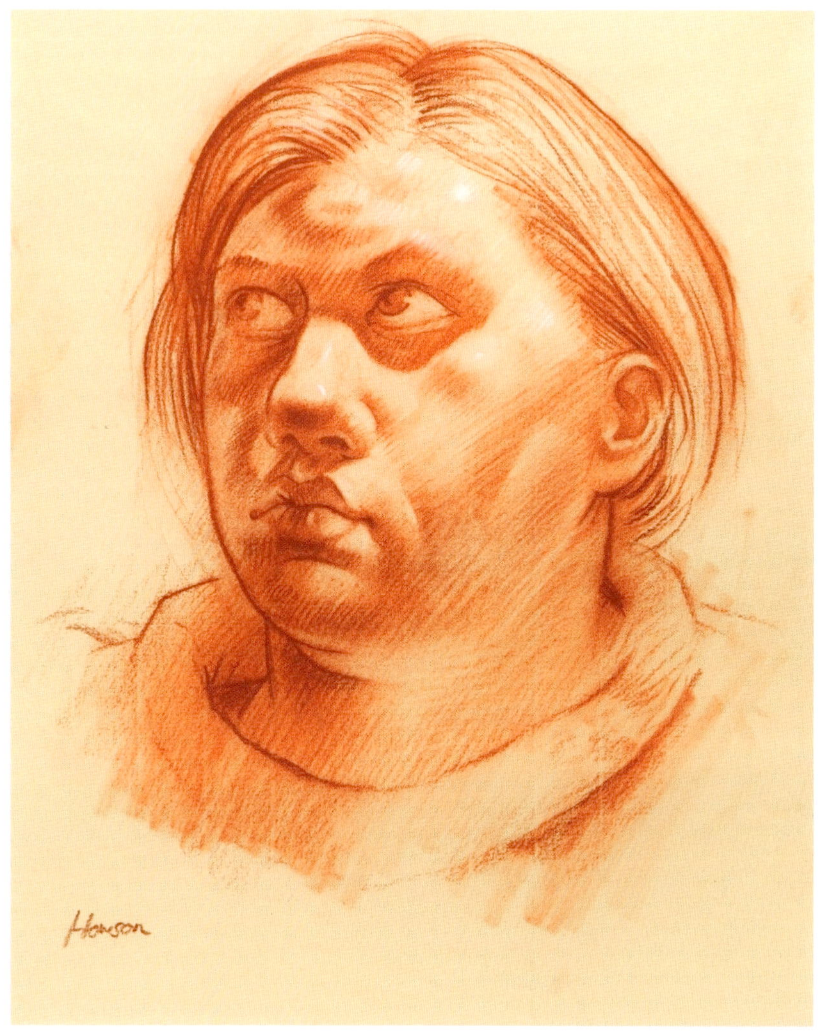

Park
1992 / conté on paper / 36.5 x 29 cm
Flowers Gallery / photograph Antonio Parente

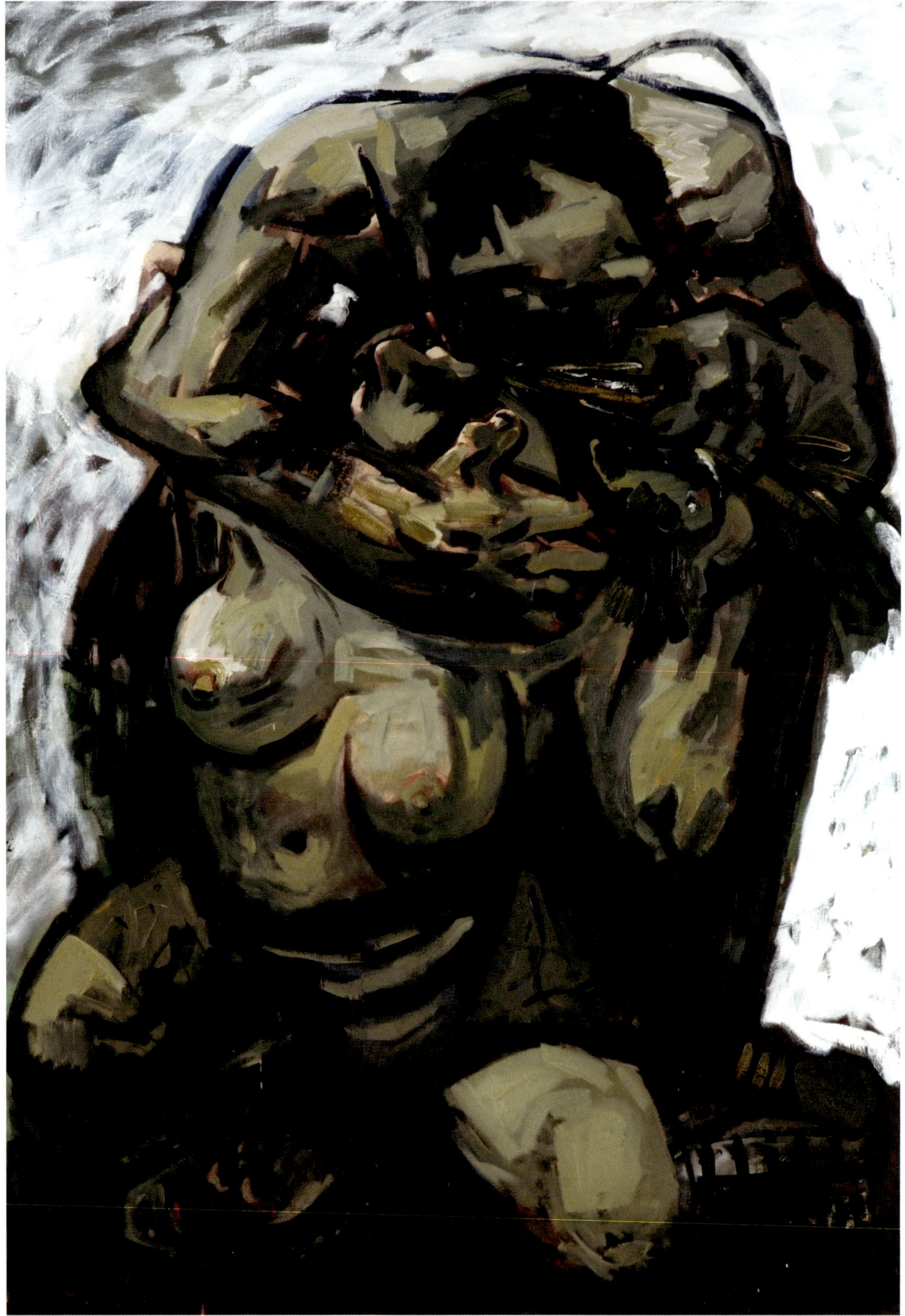

Serb and Muslim
1994 / oil on canvas / 213.5 x 152.5 cm
Aberdeen City Council (Aberdeen Archives, Gallery and Museums collections)
purchased in 1995 with assistance from the National Fund for Acquisitions and
with income from the Lyon Bequest, the Murray Fund and the Jaffrey Fund

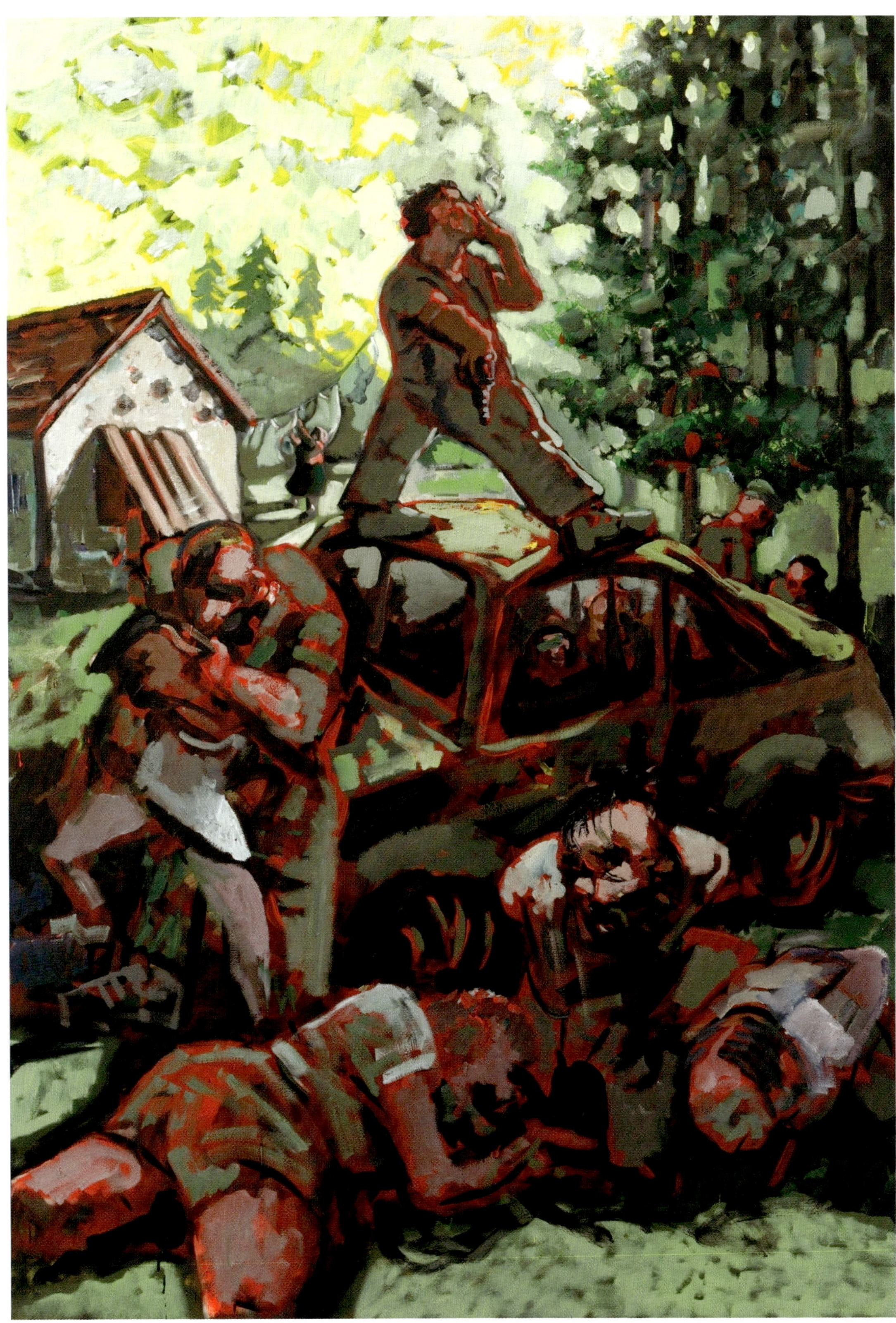

House Warming
1994 / oil on canvas / 213 x 152.5 cm
private collection / photograph Antonio Parente

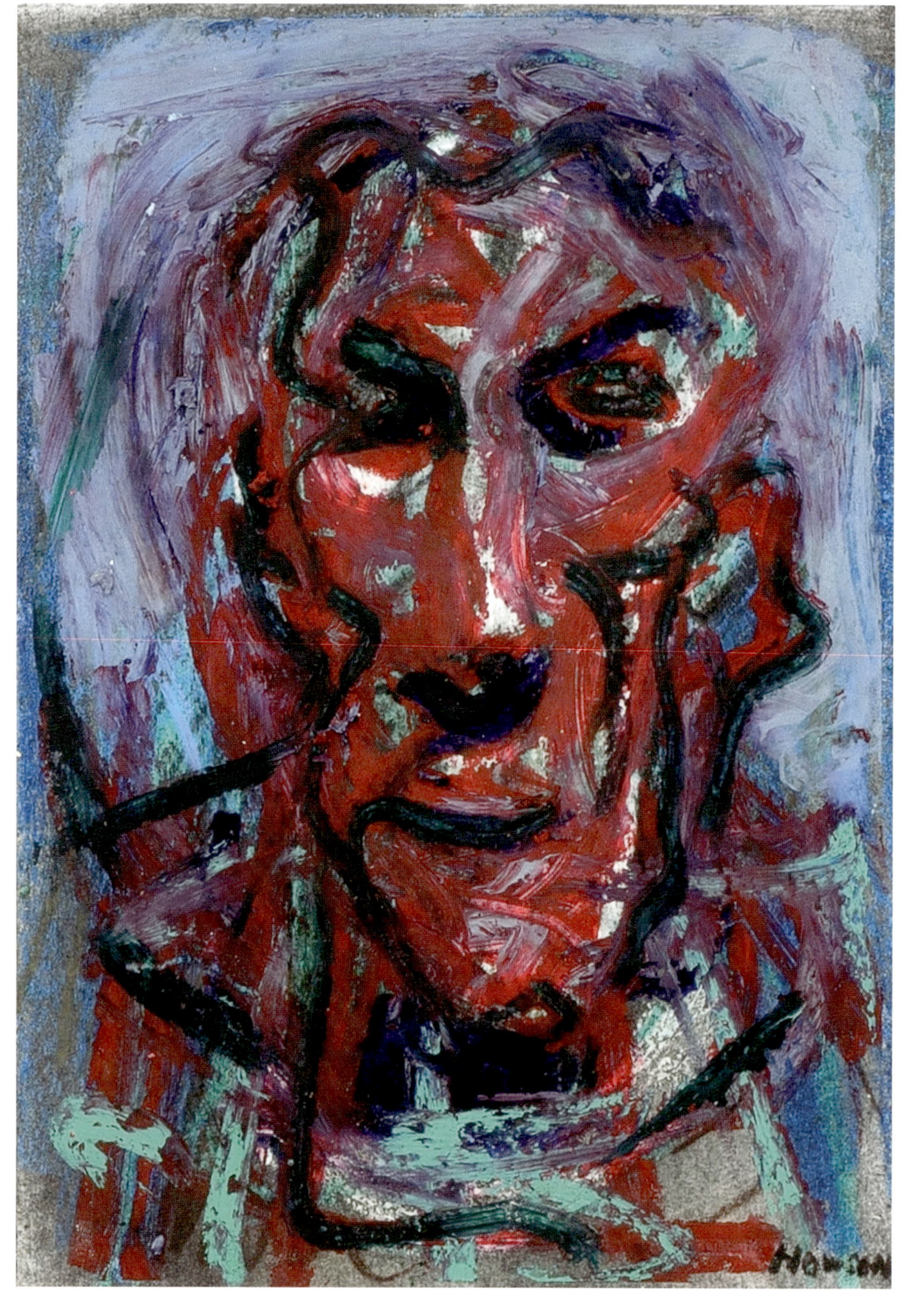

Woodsman
1994 / oil pastel on paper / 20.5 x 14.5 cm
Flowers Gallery / photograph Antonio Parente

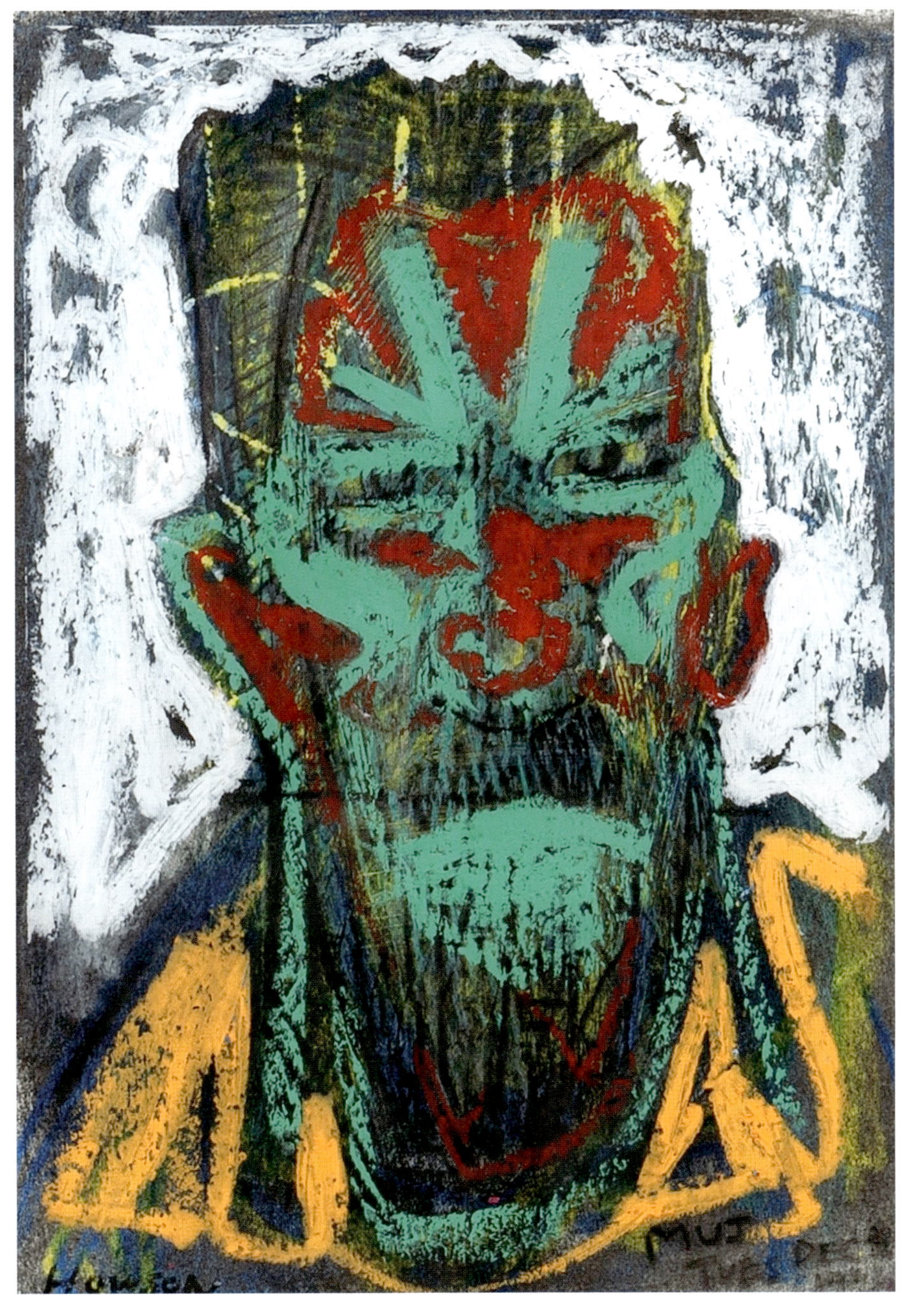

Zenica
1994 / oil pastel on paper / 20.5 x 14.5 cm
Flowers Gallery / photograph Antonio Parente

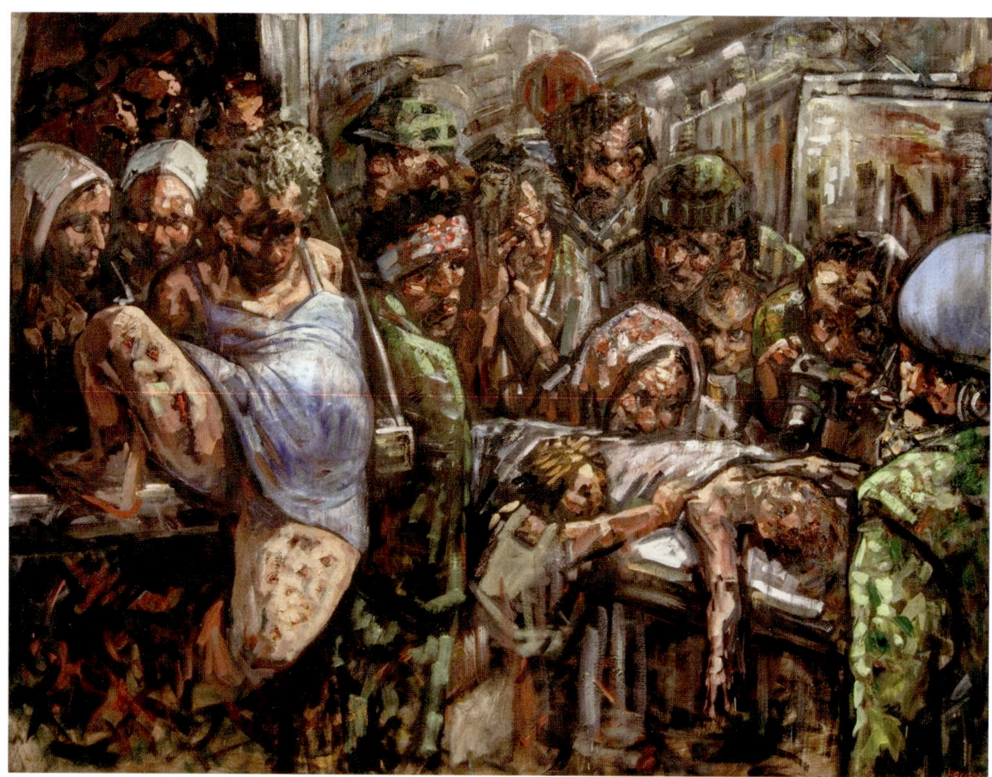

Sanctuary in Travnik
1994 / oil on canvas / 183 x 244 cm
Flowers Gallery / photograph Antonio Parente

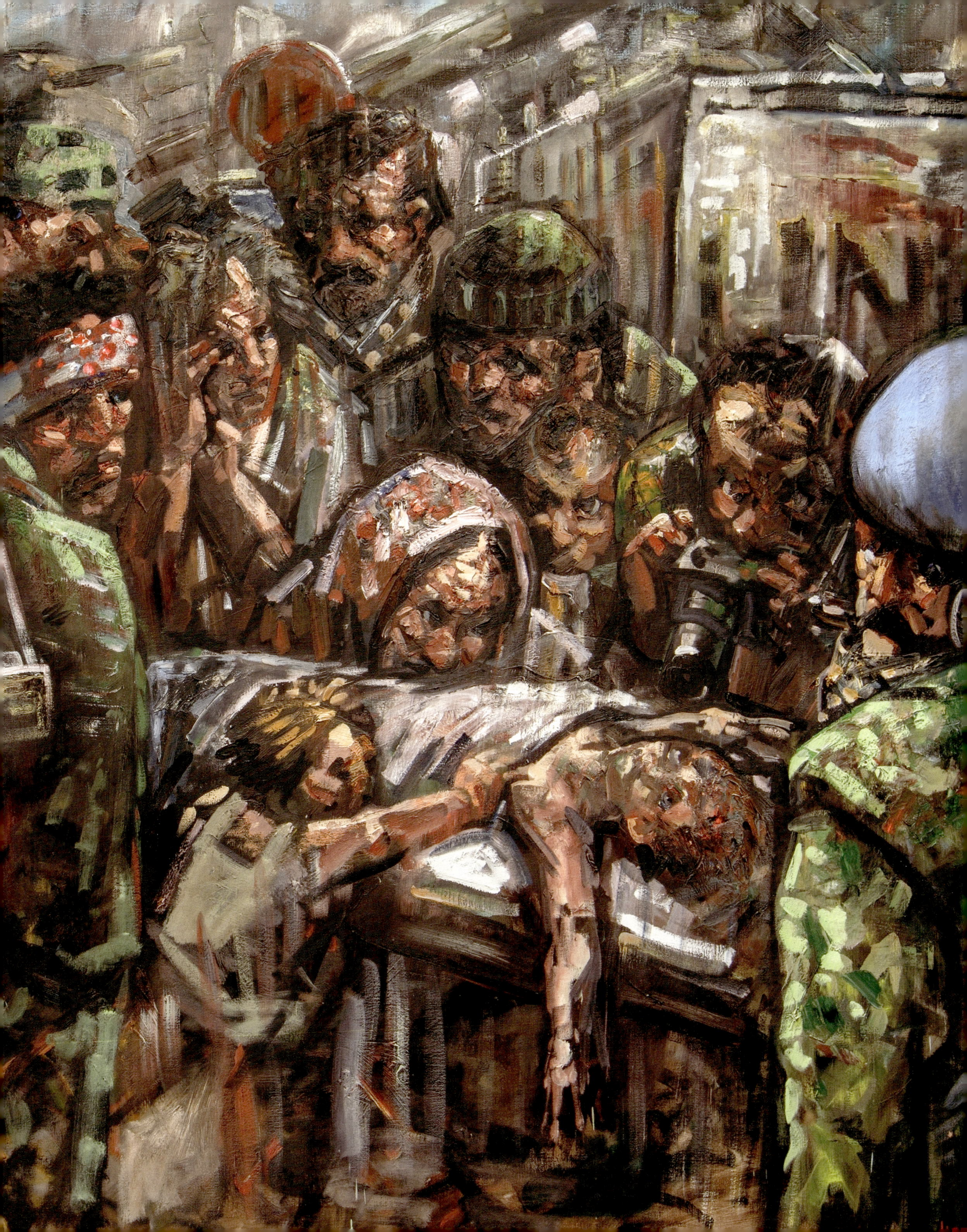

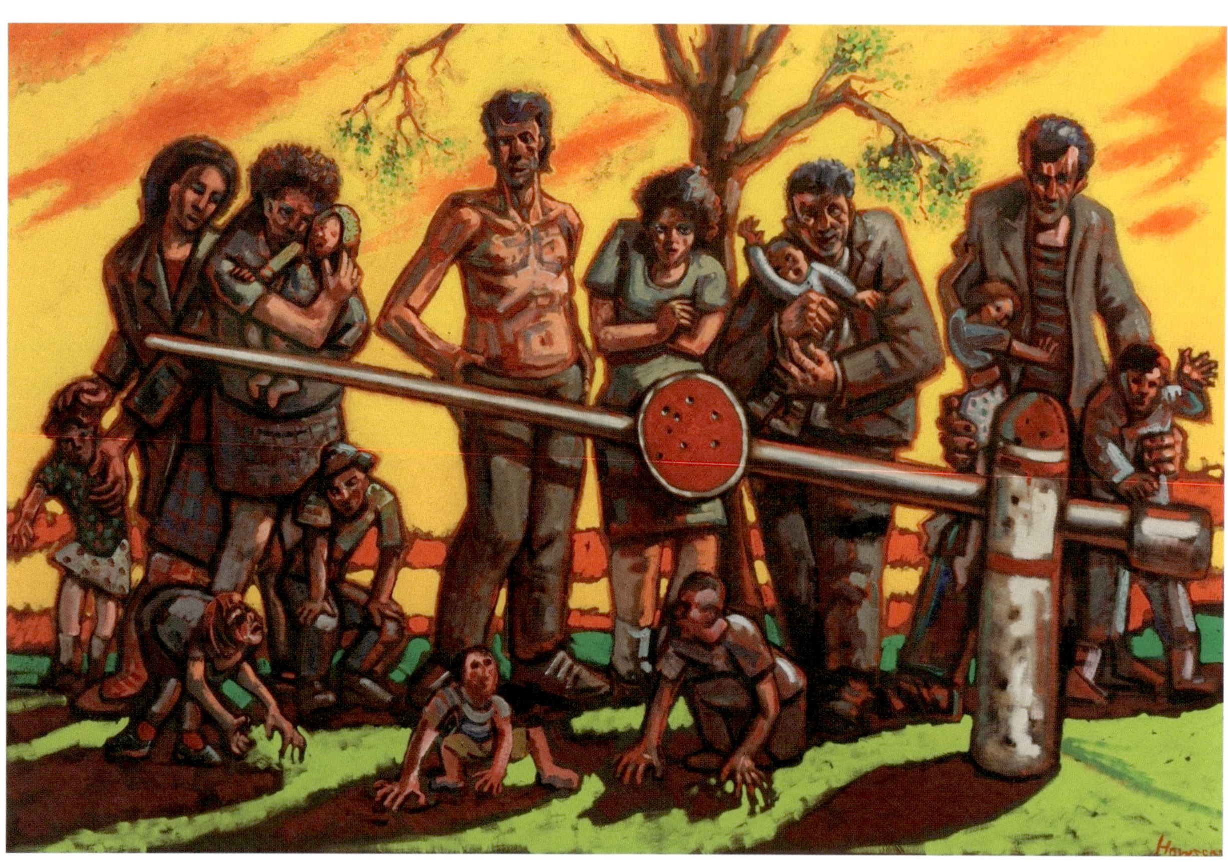

Barrier Sunset
1995 / oil on canvas / 122 x 183 cm
Flowers Gallery / photograph Antonio Parente

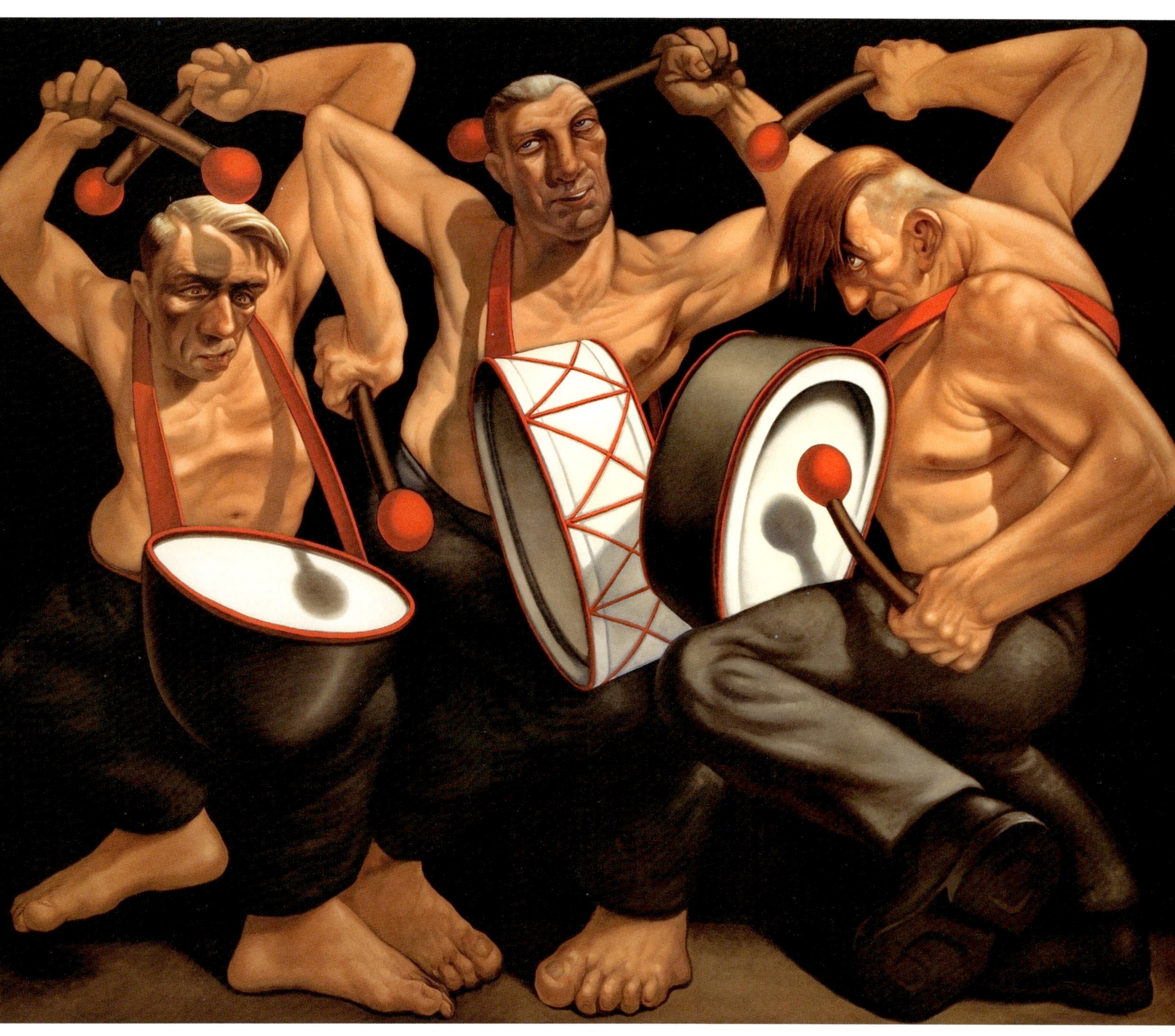

Drum
1995 / oil on canvas / 244 x 305 cm
Flowers Gallery / photograph Antonio Parente

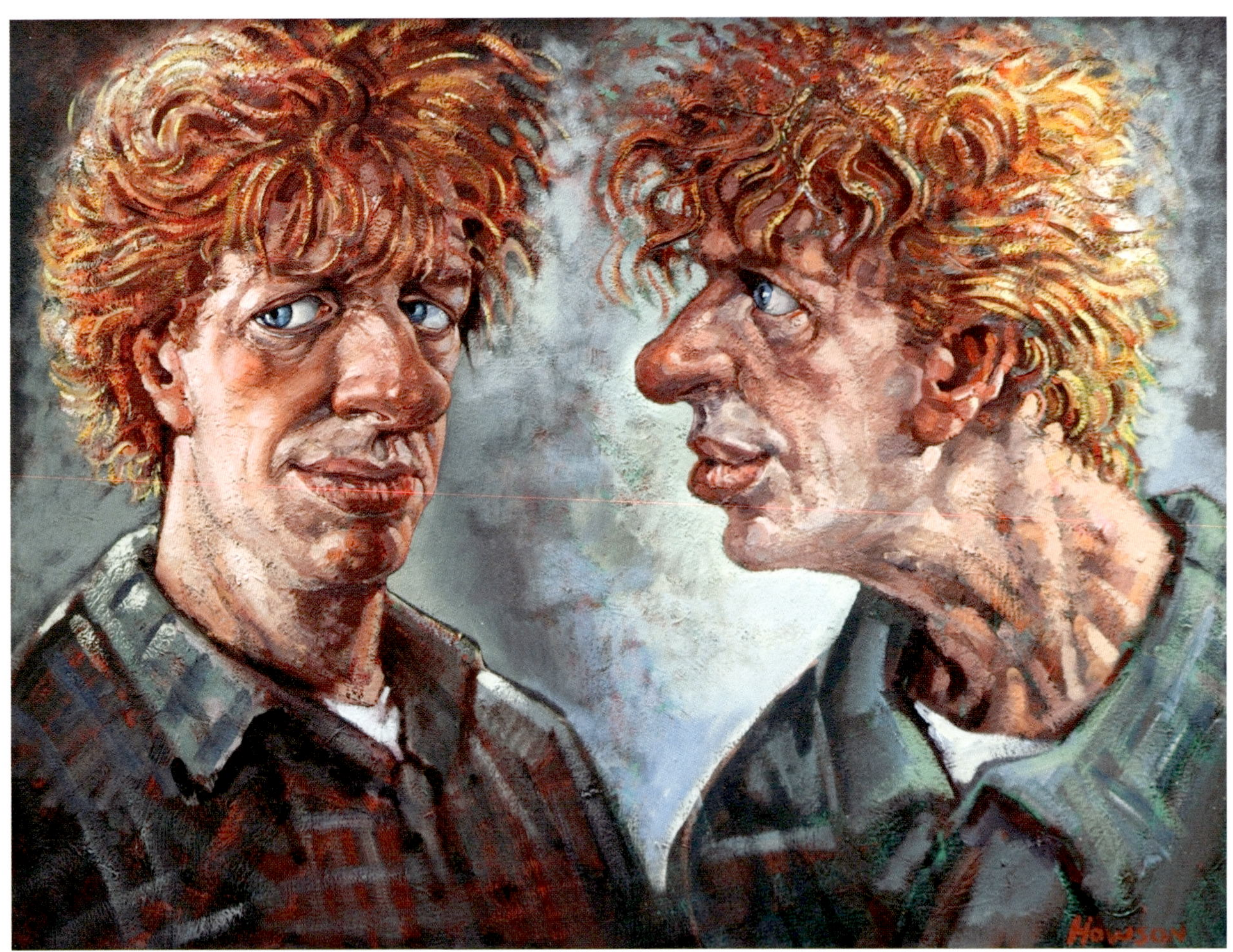

Jekyll and Hyde
1995 / oil on canvas / 91.5 x 152.5 cm
private collection

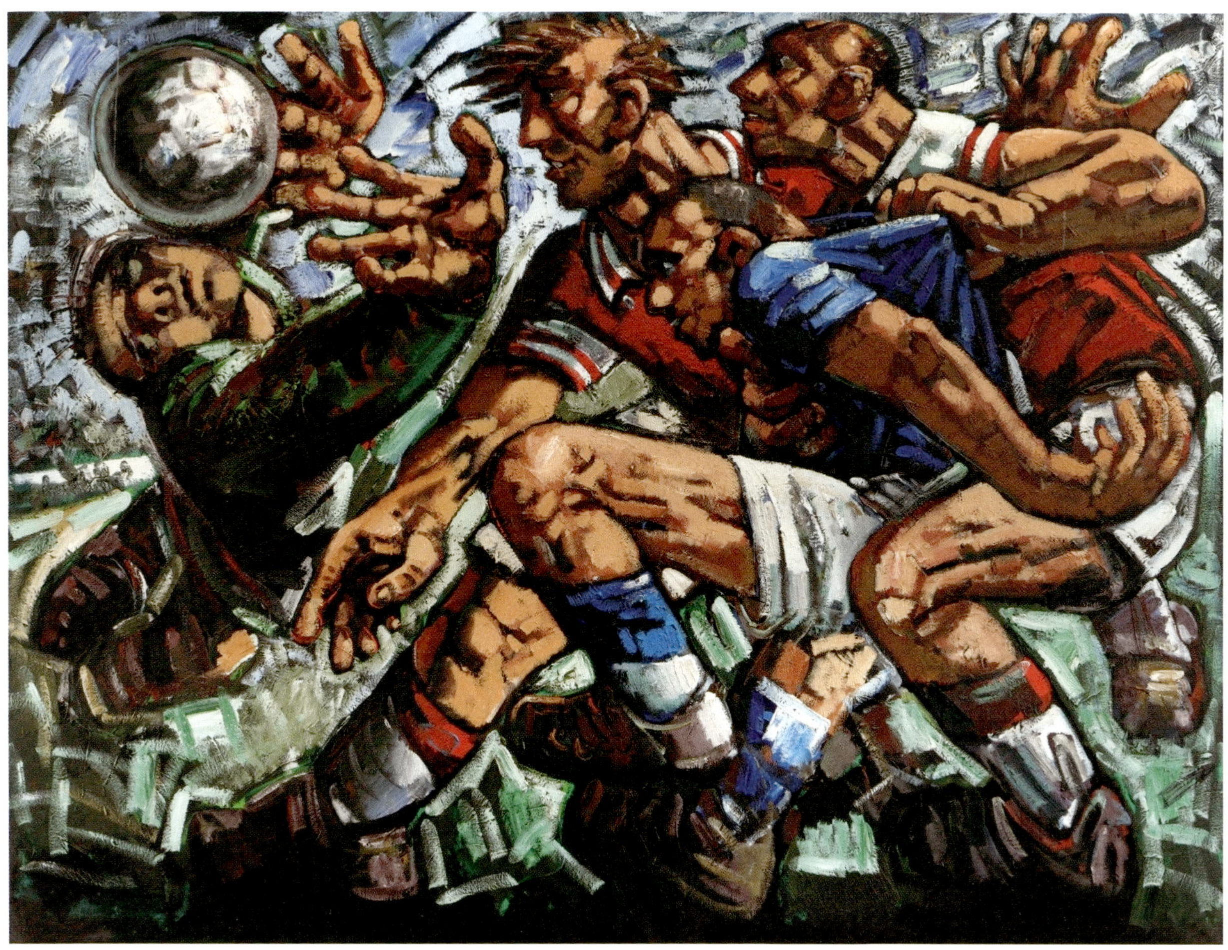

Football
1997 / oil on canvas / 183 x 245 cm
Flowers Gallery / photograph Antonio Parente

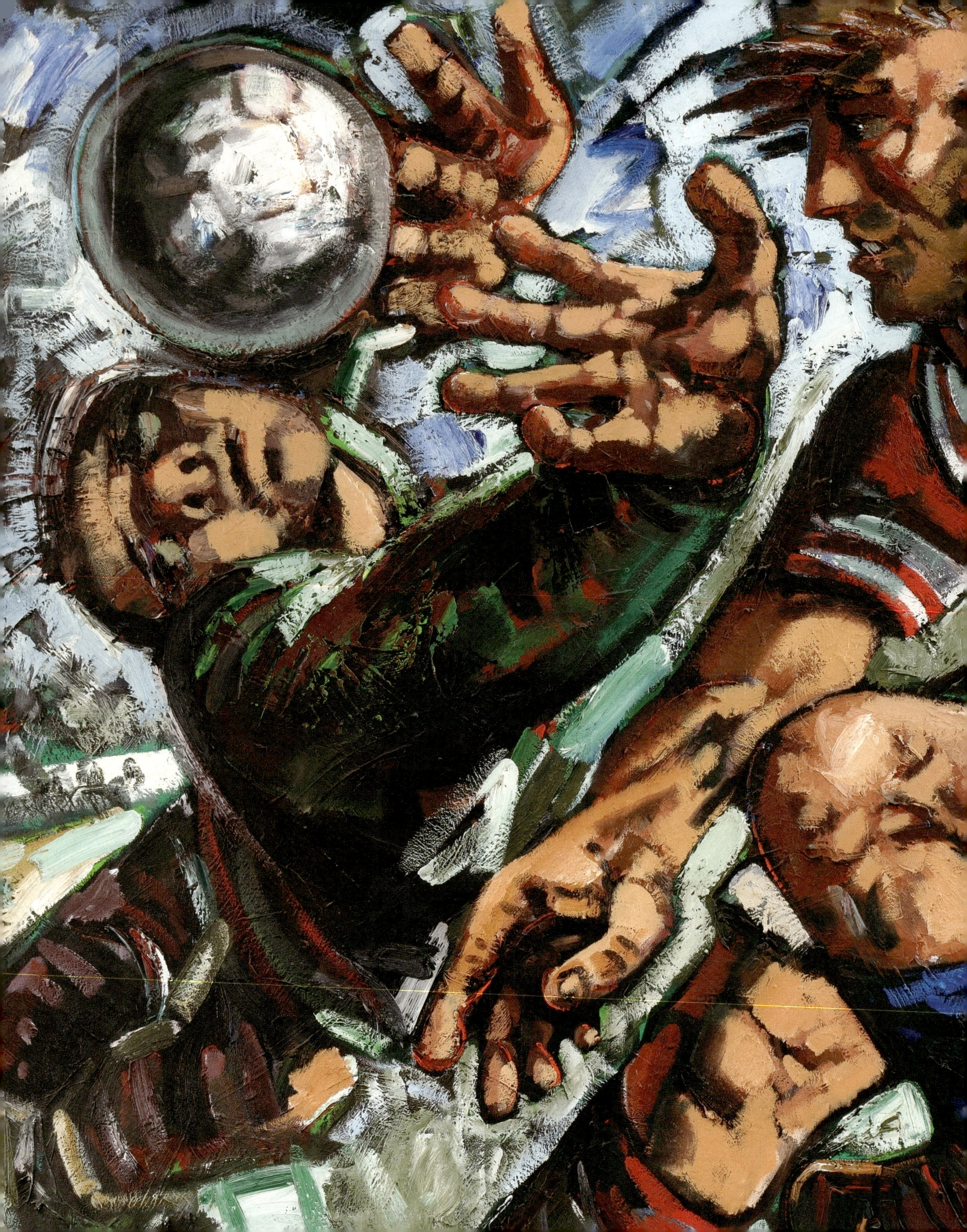

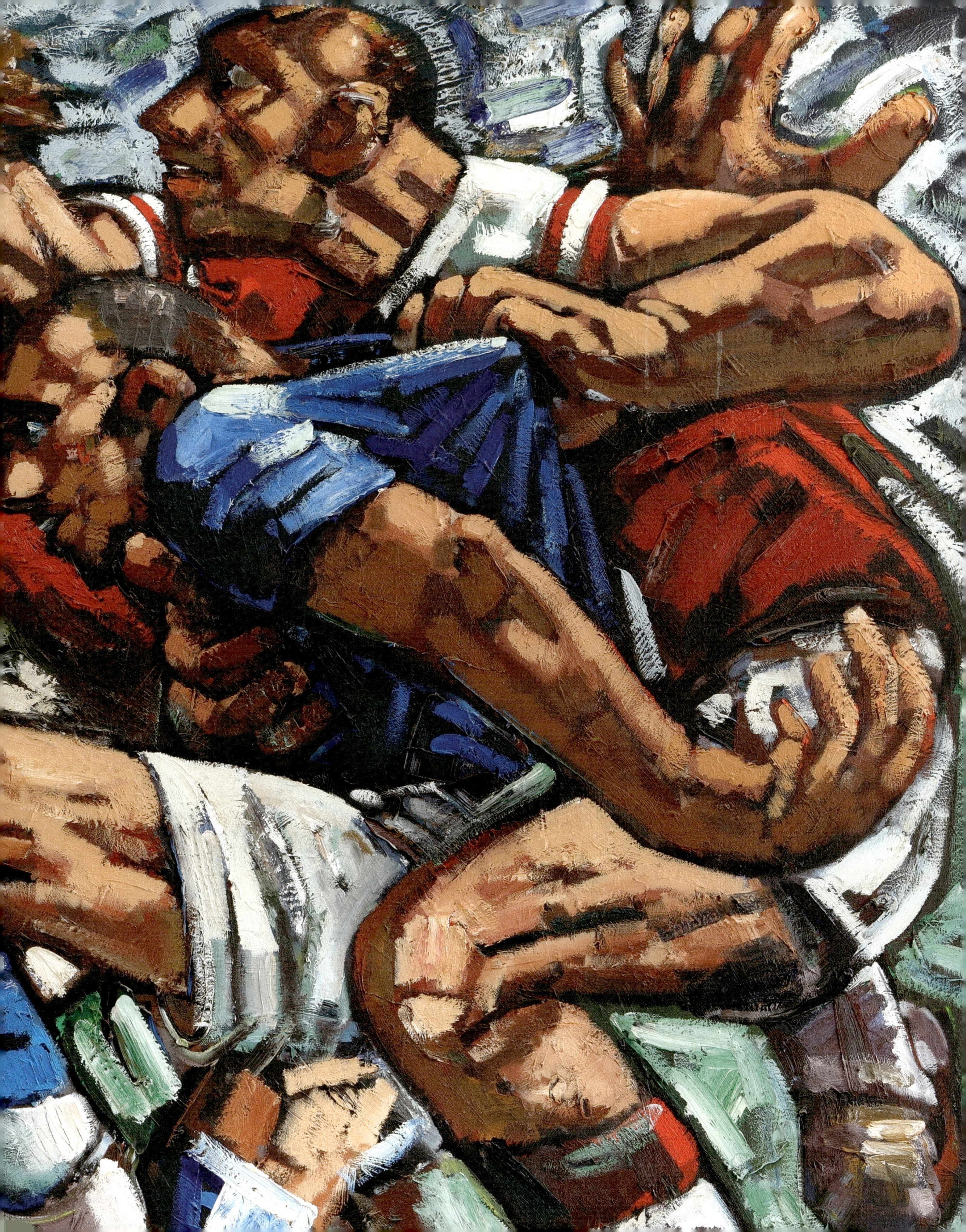

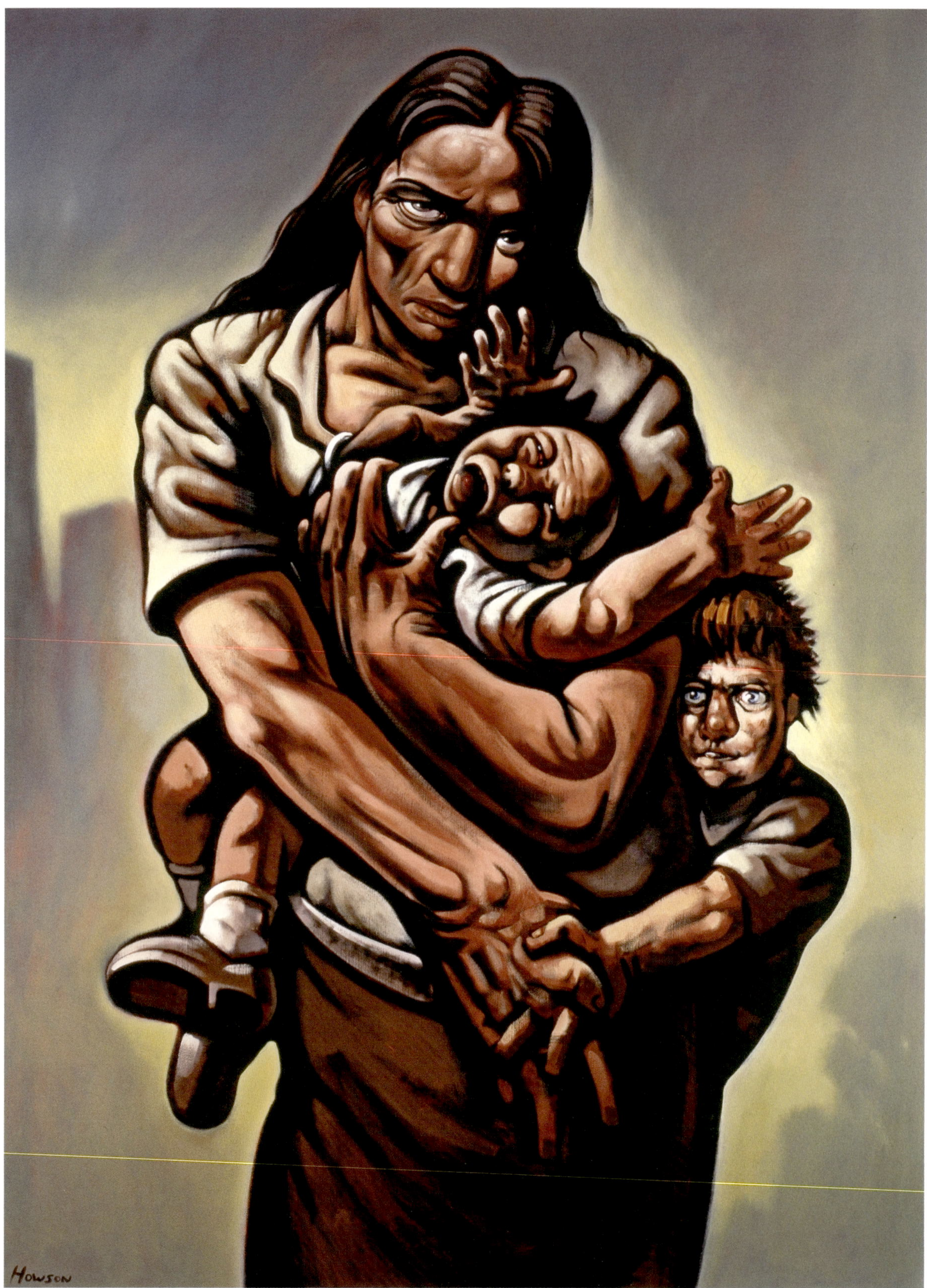

Through the Borders
1999 / oil on canvas / 183 x 138 cm
Steven Berkoff

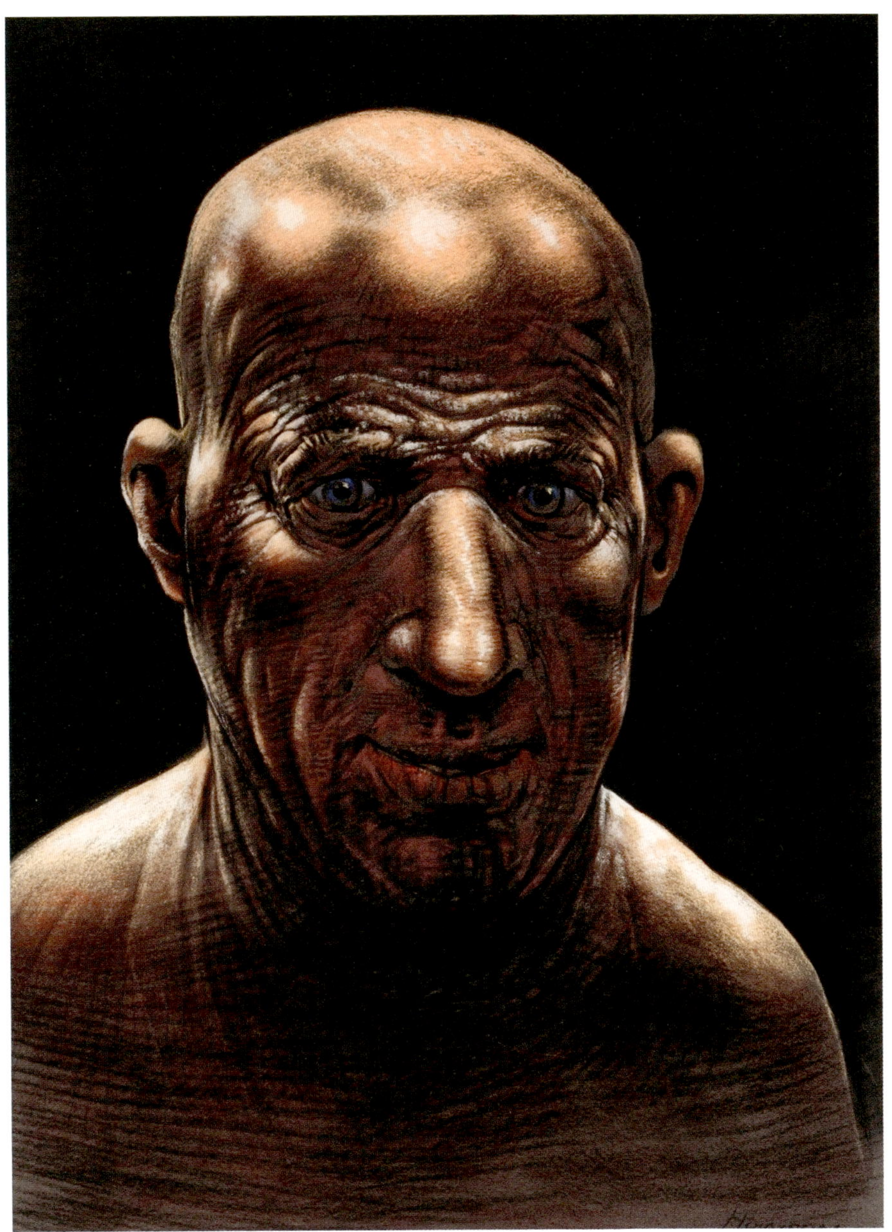

Self-Portrait Repentant
2001 / pastel on paper / 59 x 44 cm
private collection / photograph Antonio Parente

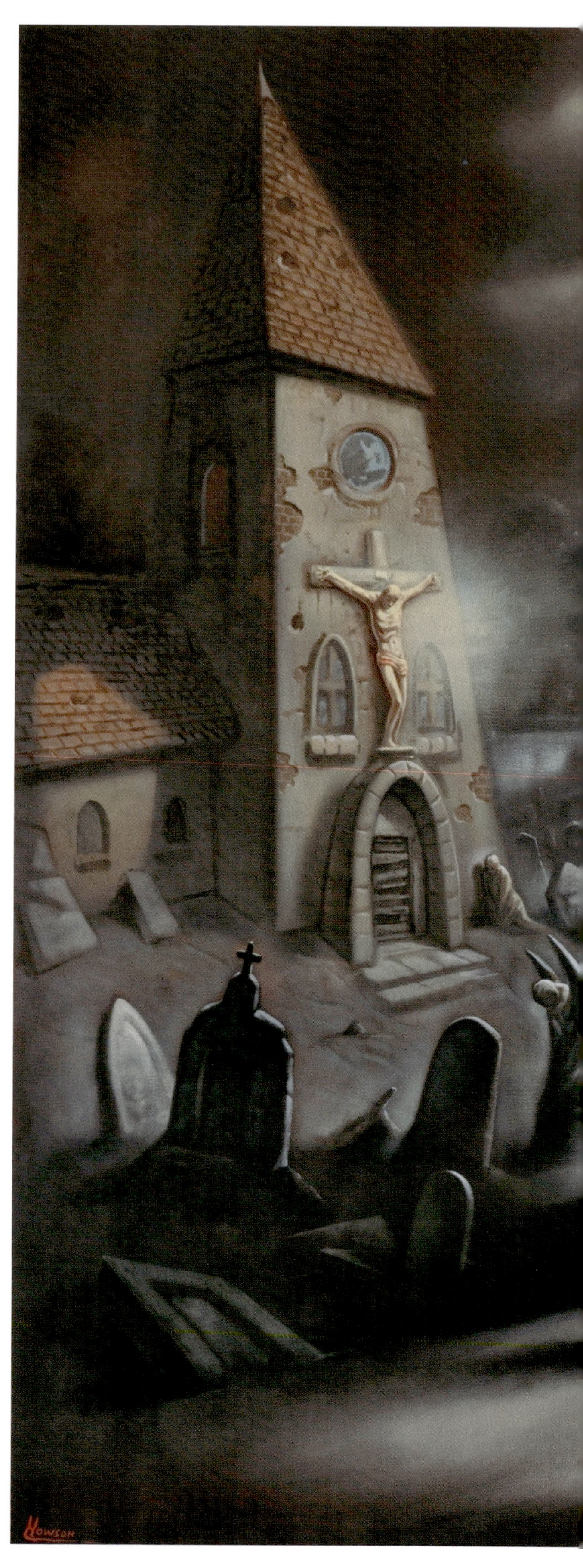

The Third Step
2001 / oil on canvas / 189 x 259 cm
Flowers Gallery / photograph Antonio Parente

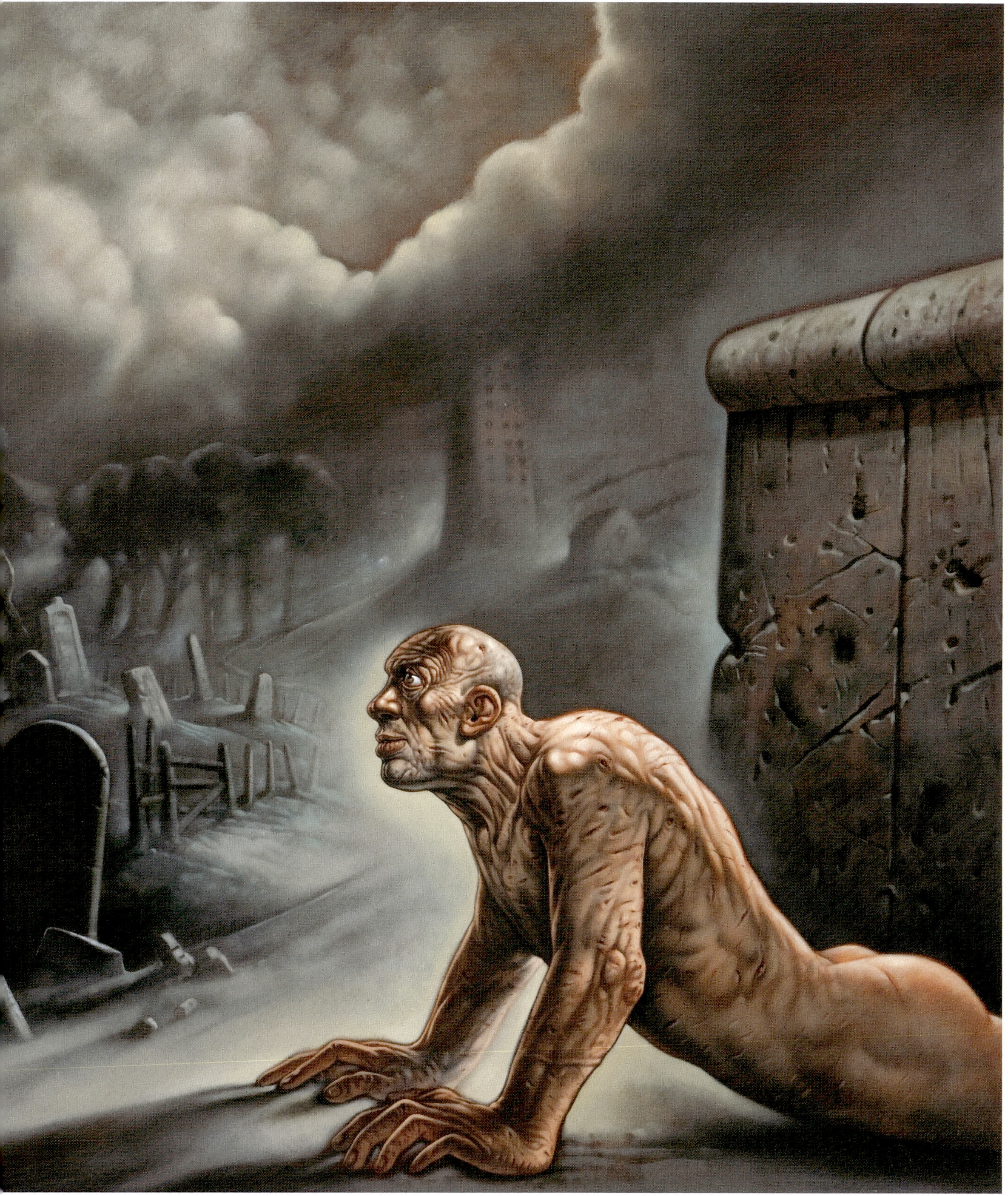

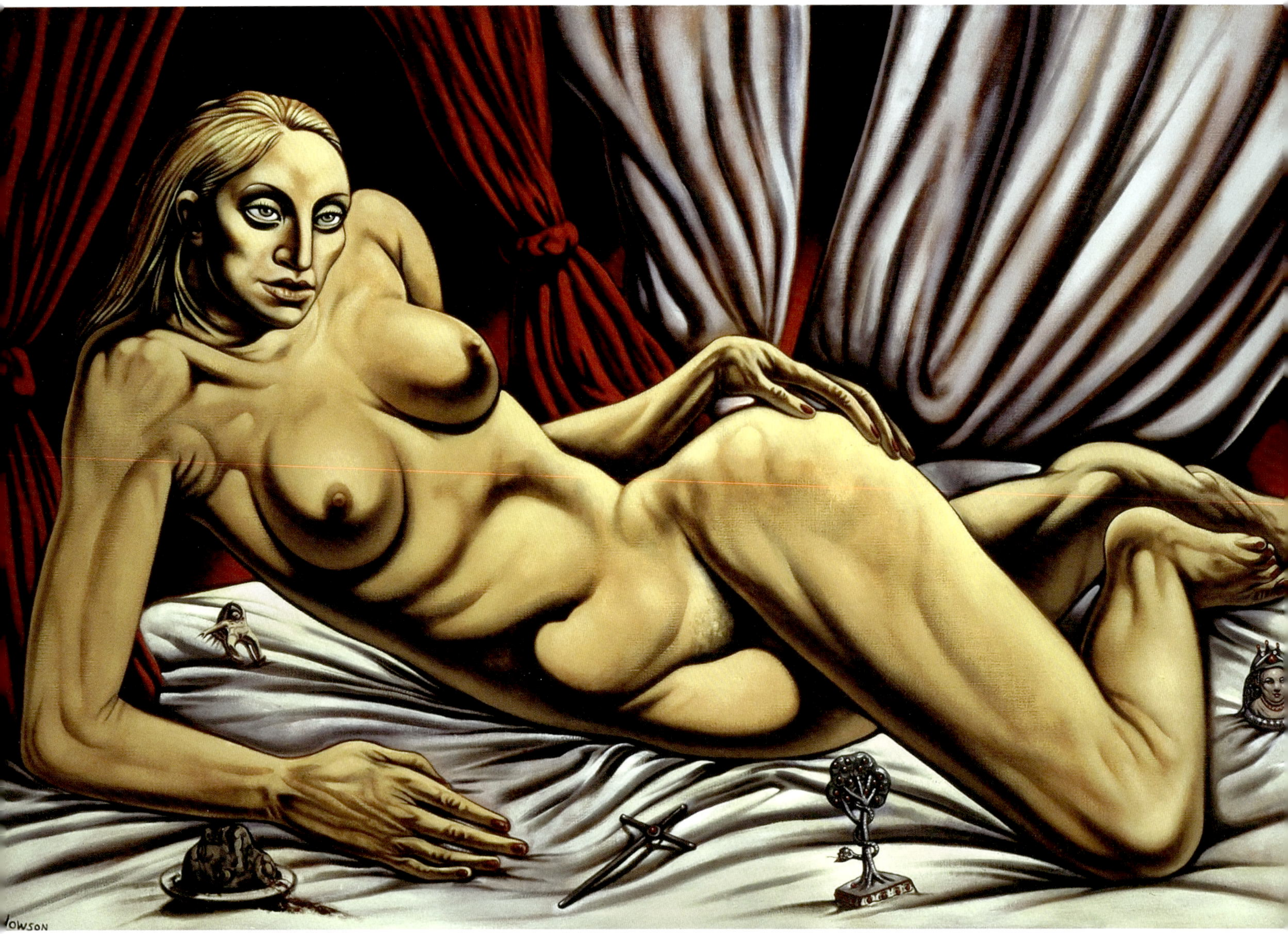

Madonna
2002 / oil on canvas / 122 x 183 cm
Matthew and Emily Flowers / photograph Antonio Parente

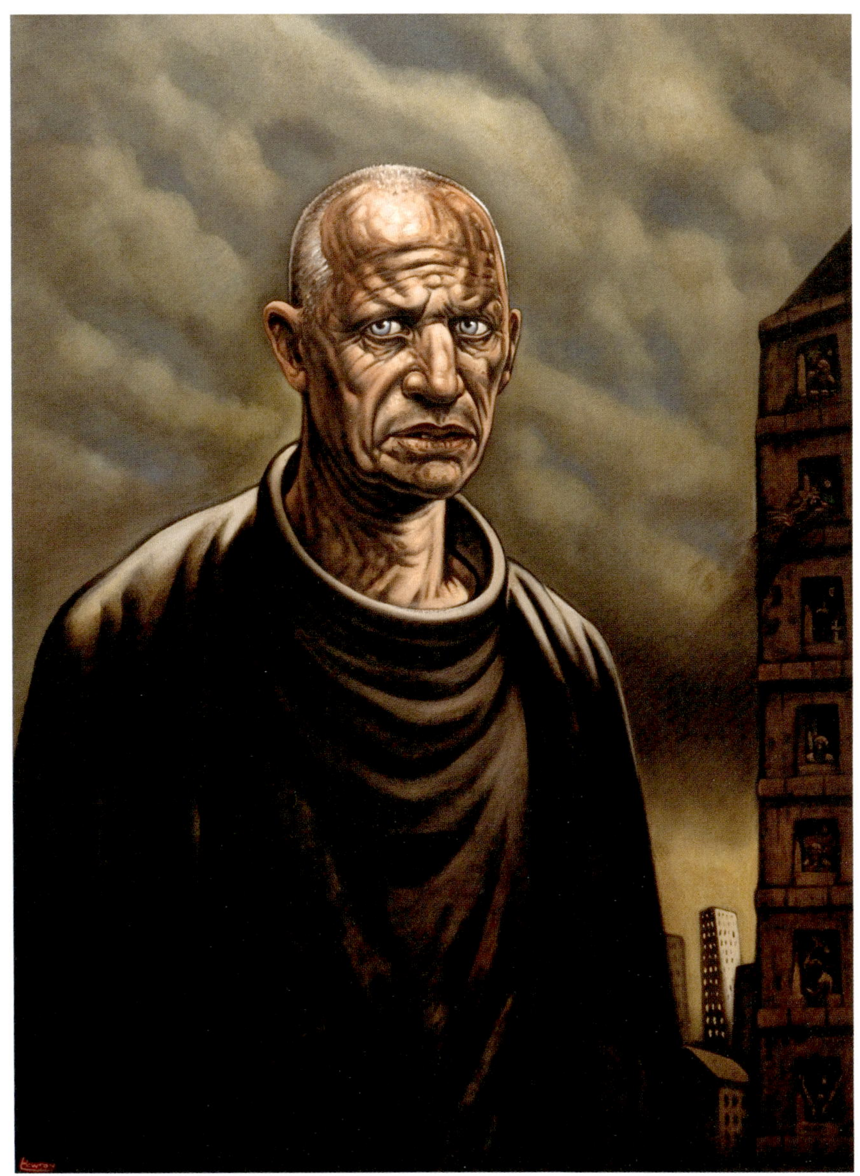

Steven Berkoff
2002 / oil on canvas / 122 x 91.5 cm
private collection / photograph Antonio Parente

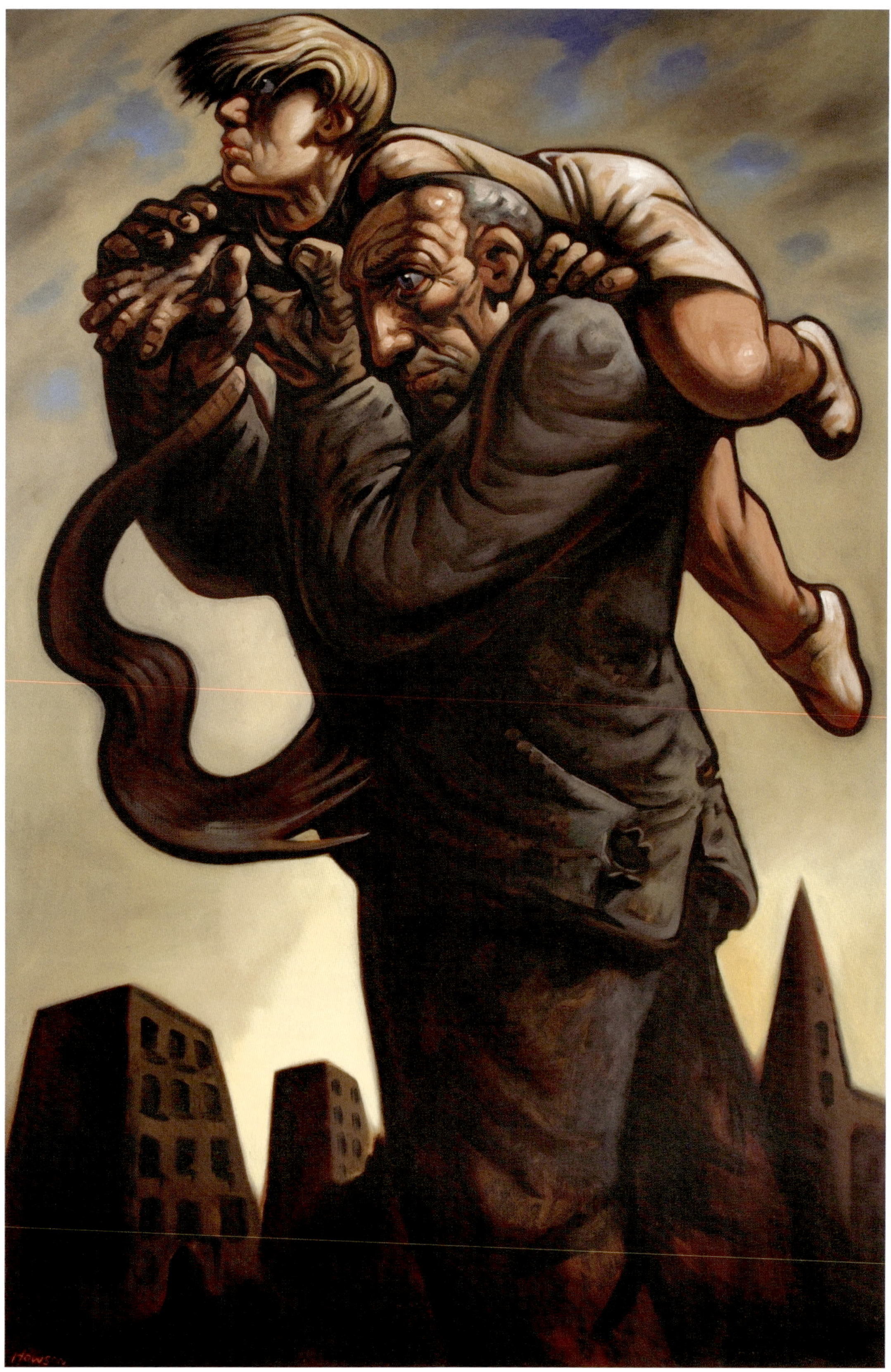

A Singular Road
2001 / oil on canvas / 183 x 125 cm
Anton Bilton / photograph Antonio Parente

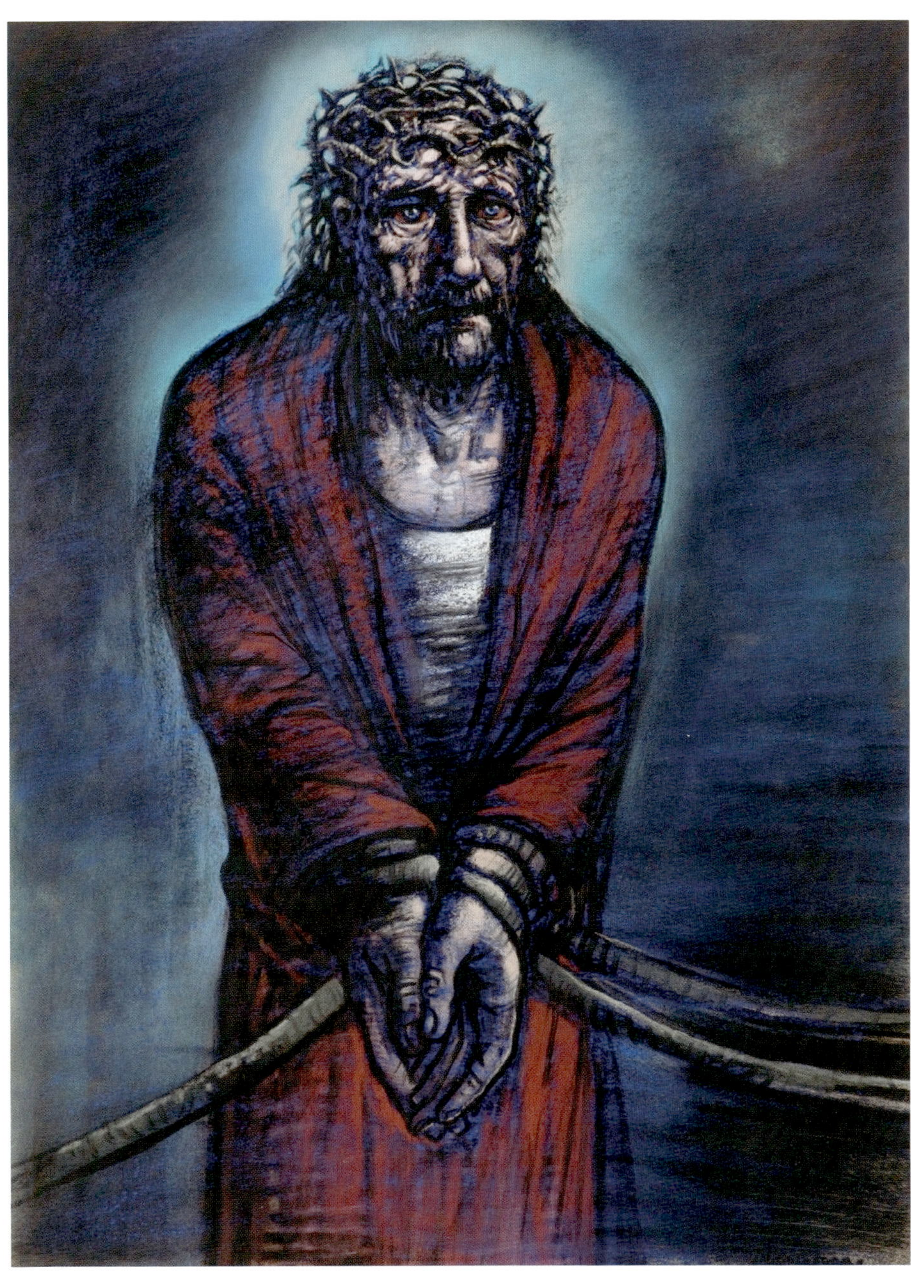

Study for Ecce Homo V
2003 / pastel and charcoal on paper / 60 x 44.5 cm
Flowers Gallery / photograph Antonio Parente

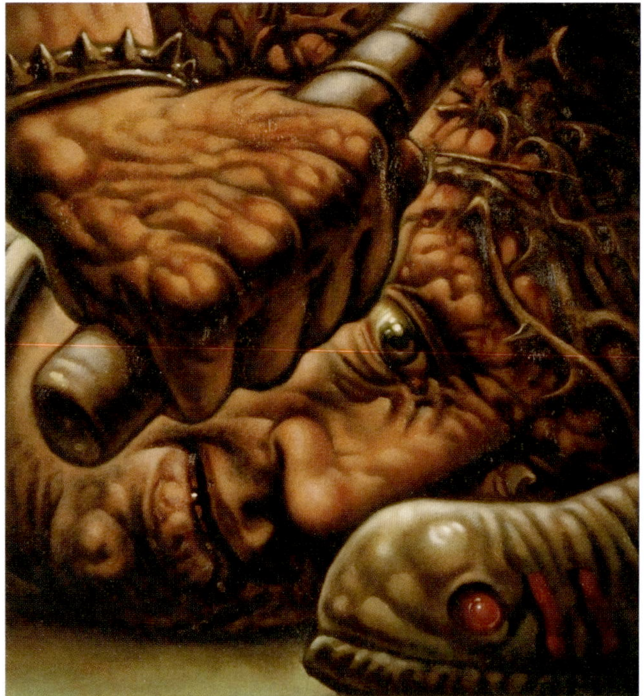

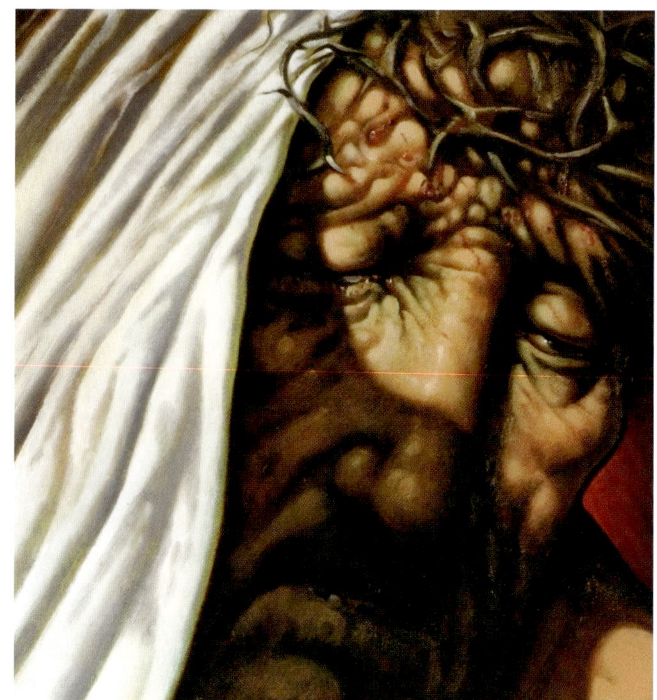

'Stations of the Cross'
Jesus Falls for the First Time
2003 / oil on board / 22 x 21 cm
John J. Studzinski CBE

'Stations of the Cross'
Veronica Cleanses the Face of Jesus
2003 / oil on board / 22 x 21 cm
John J. Studzinski CBE

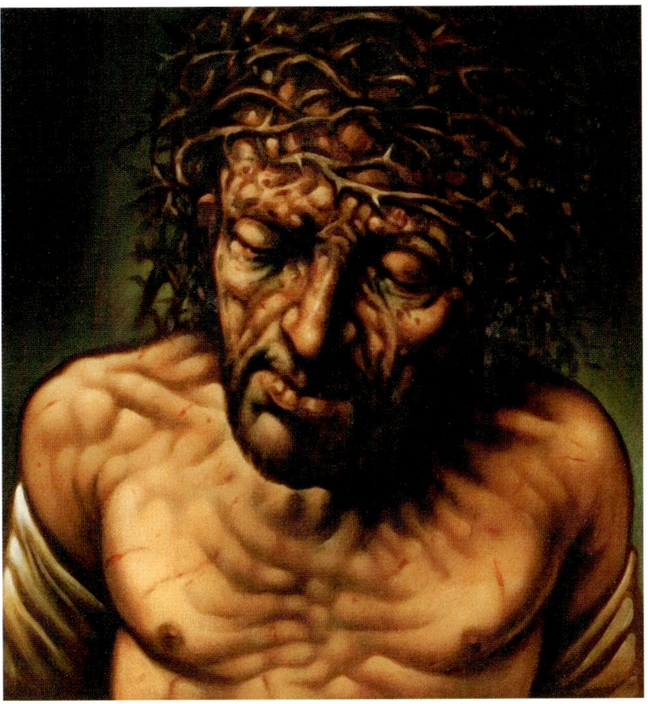

'Stations of the Cross'
Jesus Is Stripped of His Garments
2003 / oil on board / 22 x 21 cm
John J. Studzinski CBE

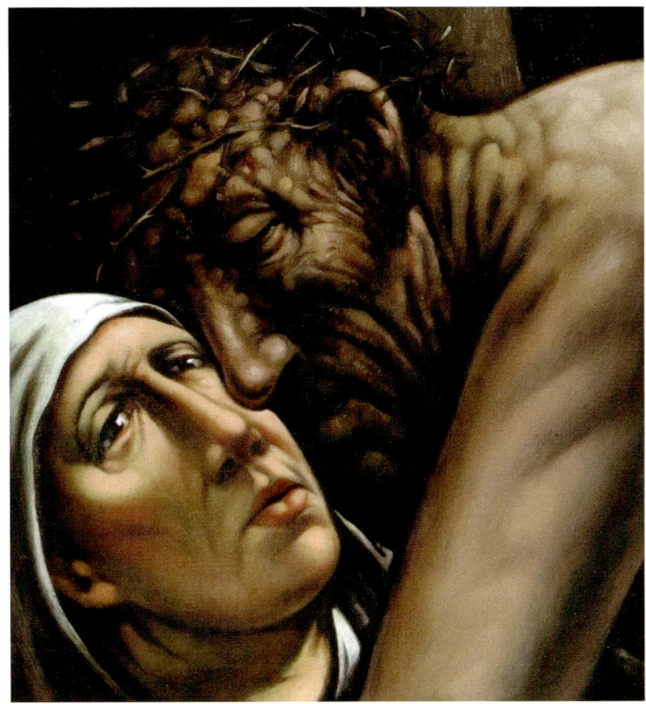

'Stations of the Cross'
Jesus Is Taken Down from the Cross
2003 / oil on board / 22 x 21 cm
John J. Studzinski CBE

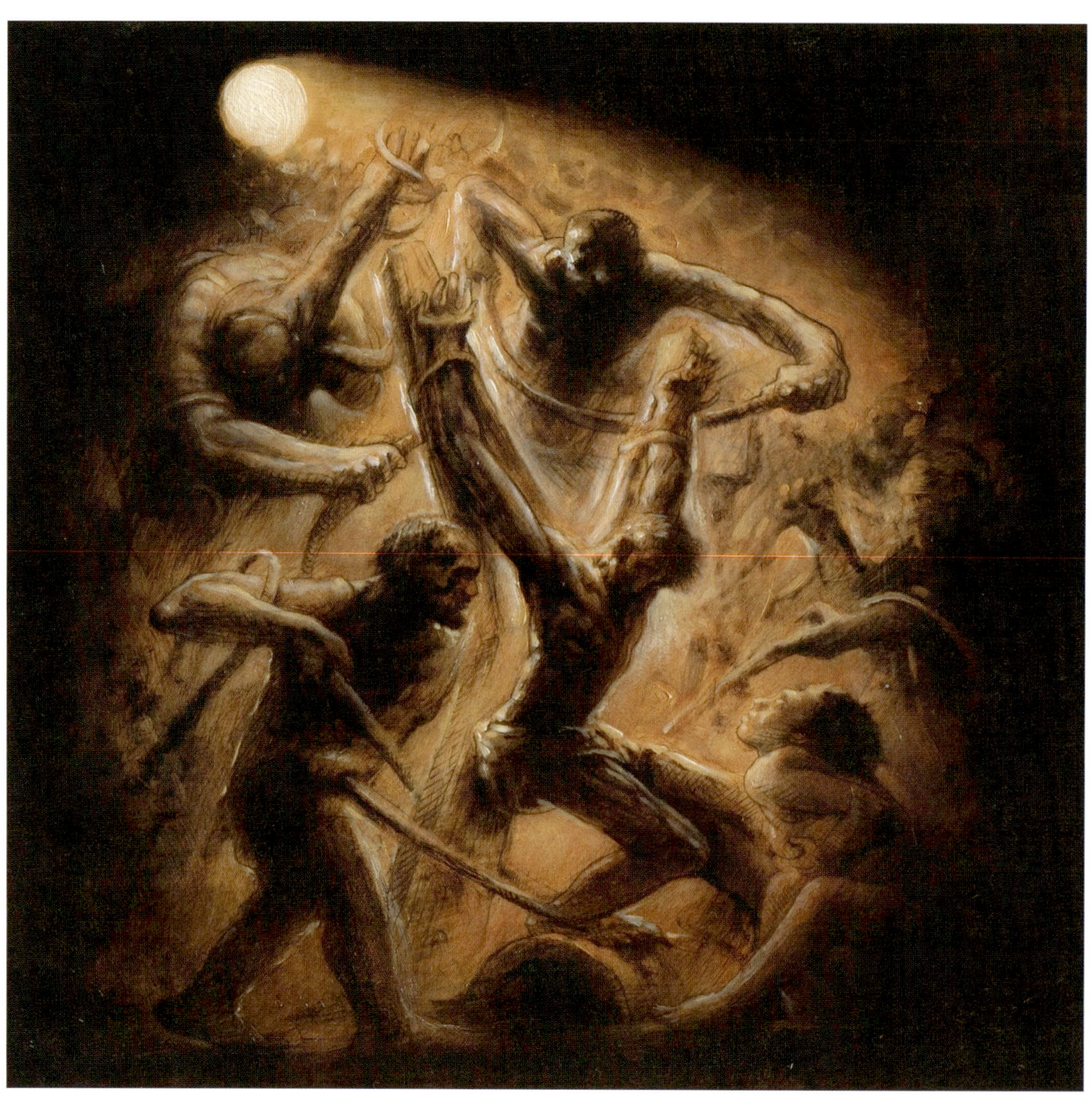

Backstreet Crucifixion (study)
2006 / oil on gessoed panel / 20 x 21 cm
City Art Centre, Edinburgh Museums and Galleries / photograph Antonia Reeve

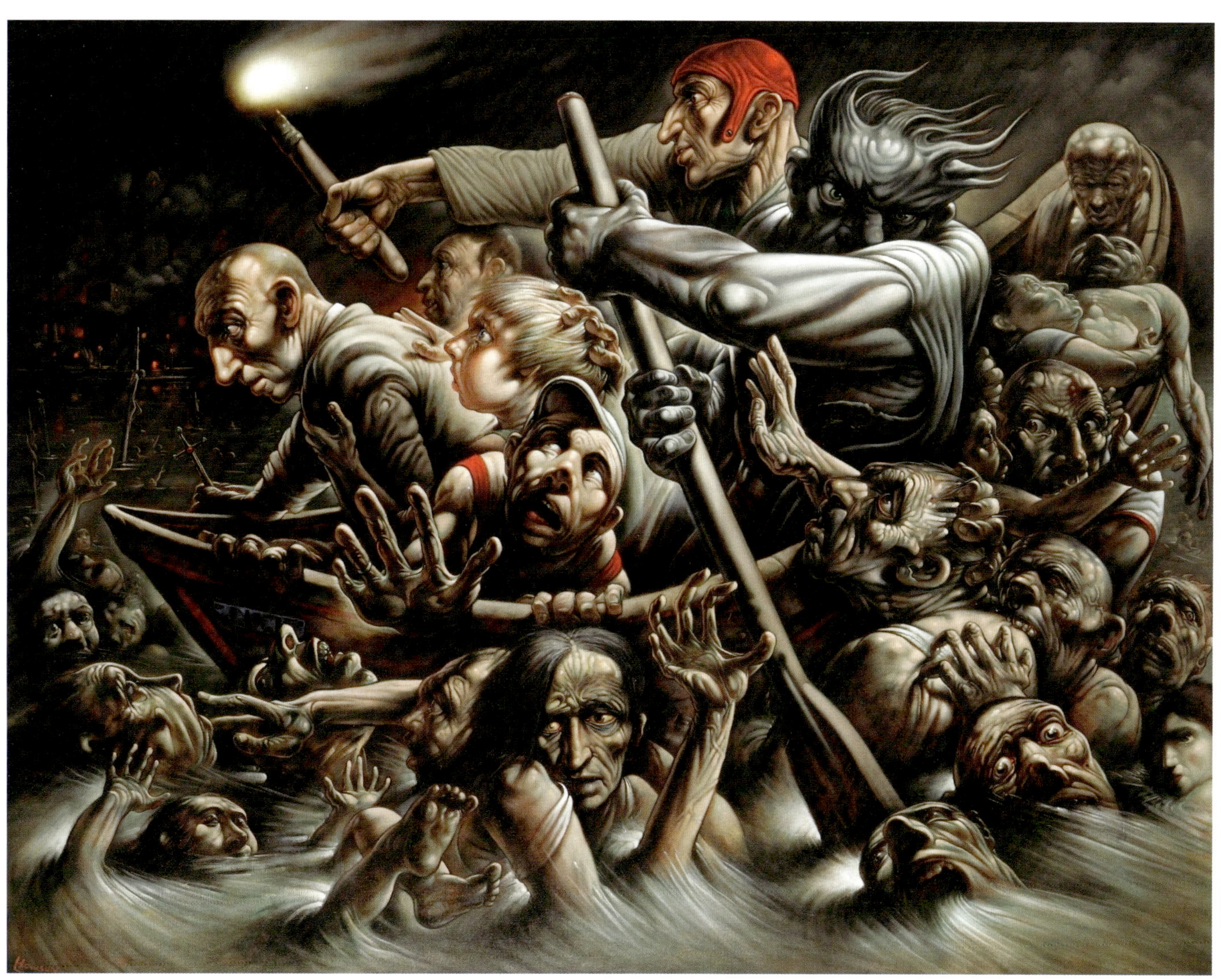

Acheron
2005 / oil on canvas / 182 x 236 cm
private collection / photograph Antonio Parente

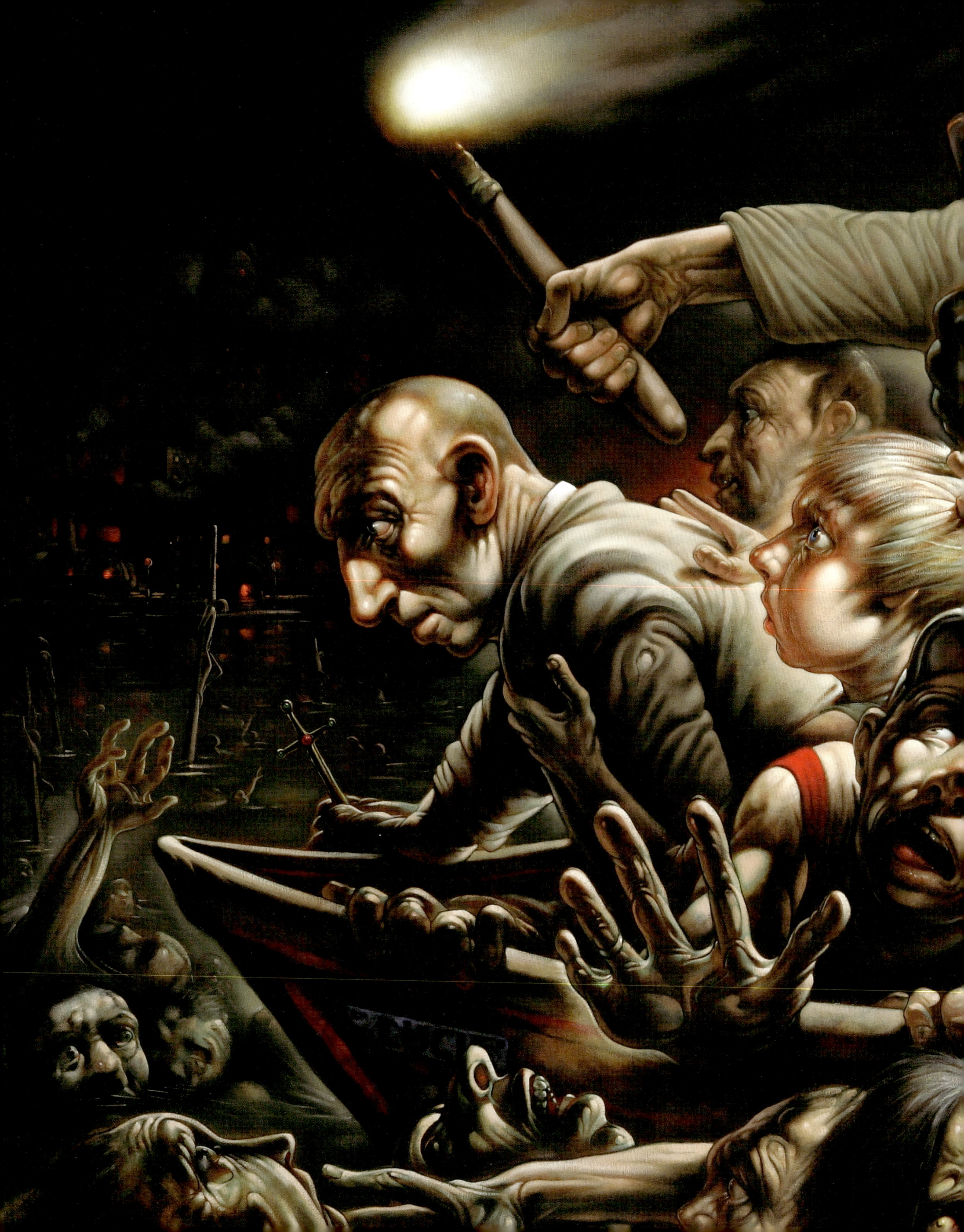

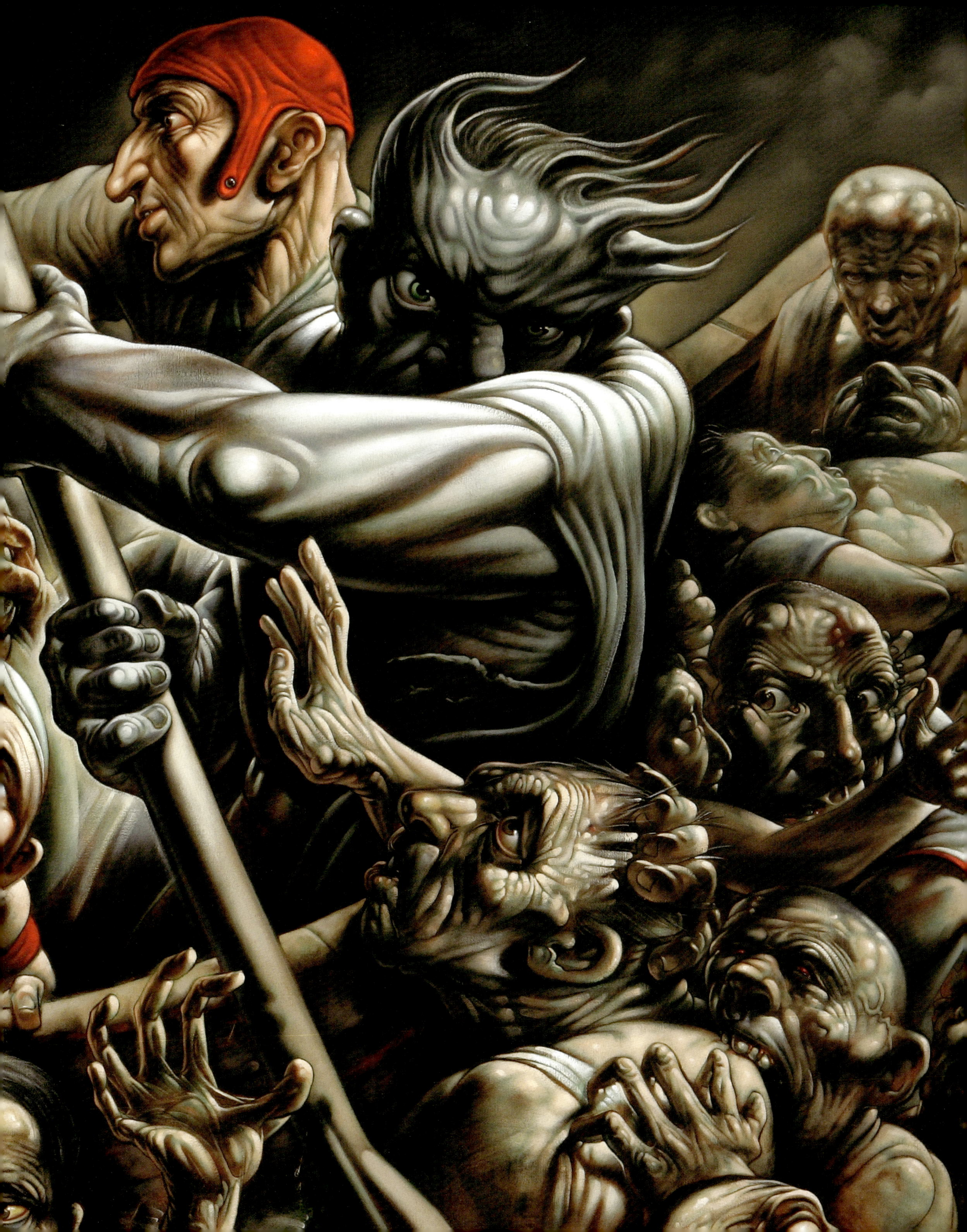

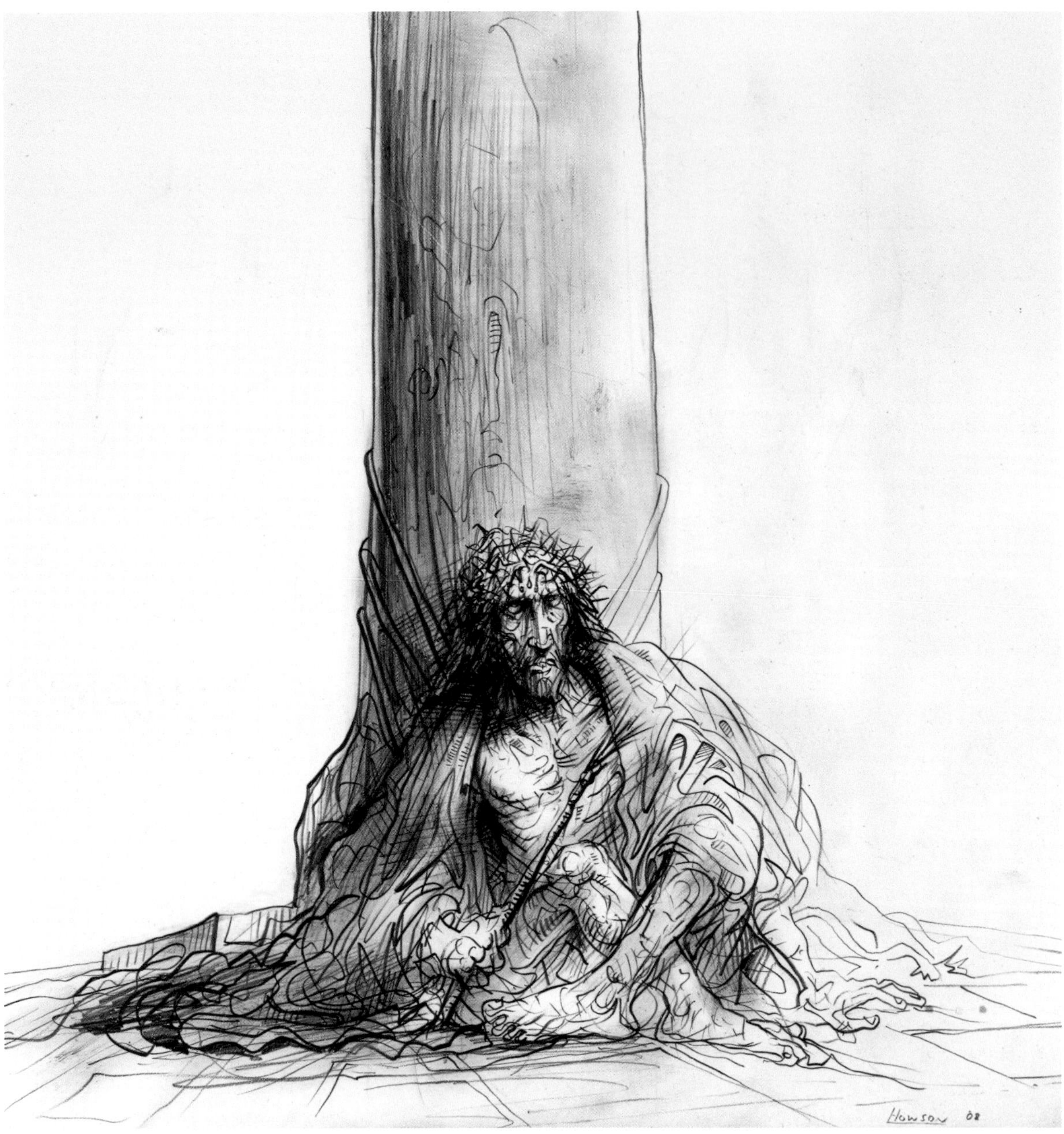

King of the Jews II
2008 / pencil on gessoed panel / 21.5 x 21 cm
private collection, Switzerland / photograph Antonio Parente

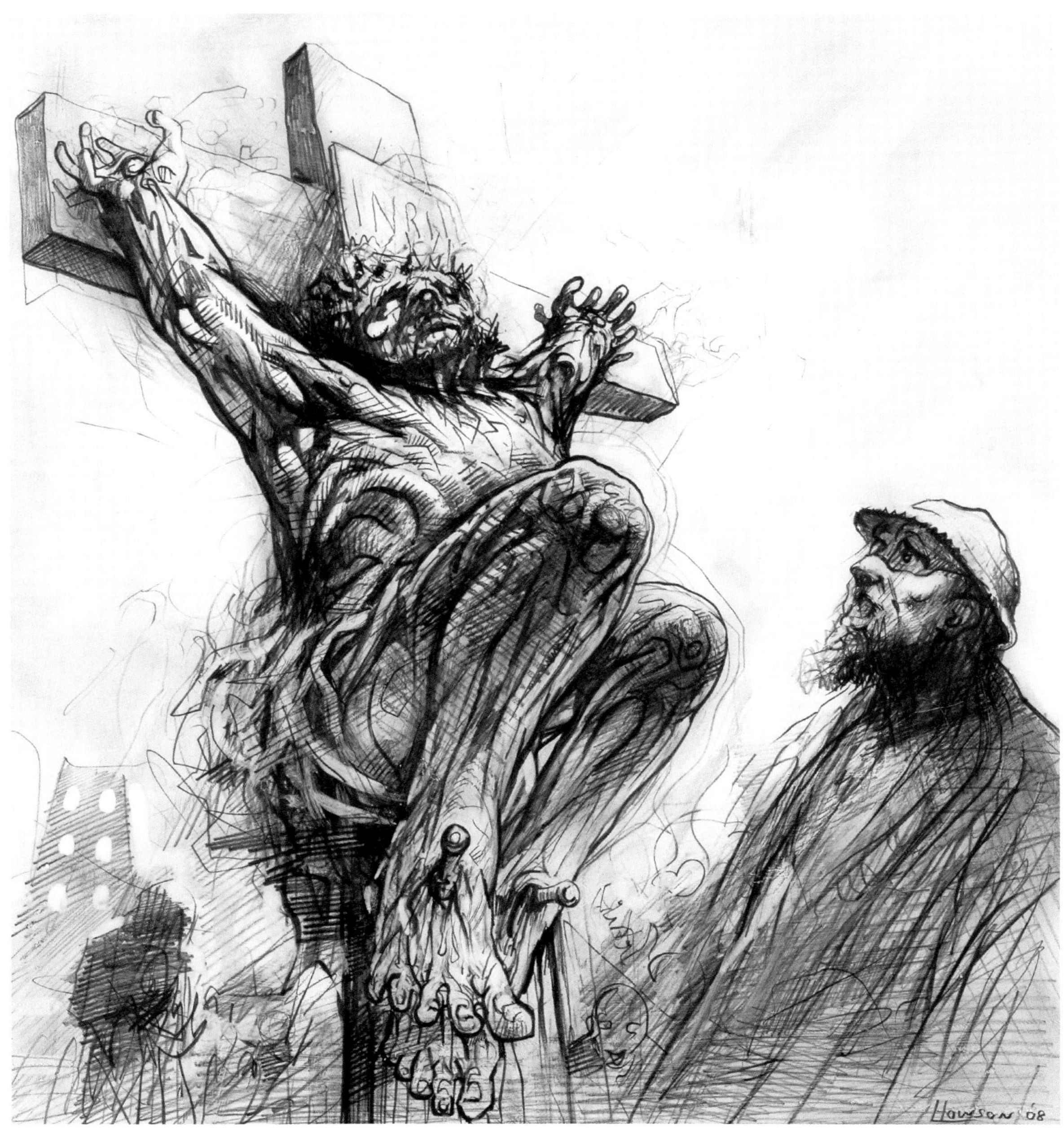

Centurion
2008 / pencil on gessoed panel / 21.5 x 21 cm
private collection, Switzerland / photograph Antonio Parente

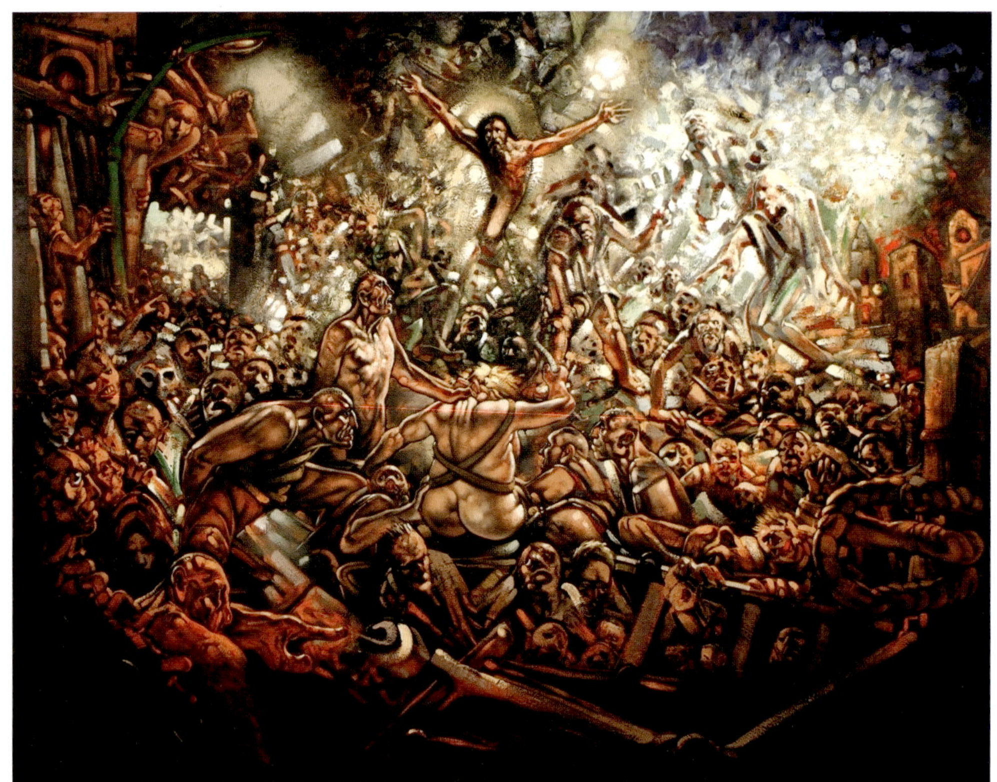

Hades IV
2011 / oil on canvas / 182 x 236 cm
private collection / photograph Antonio Parente

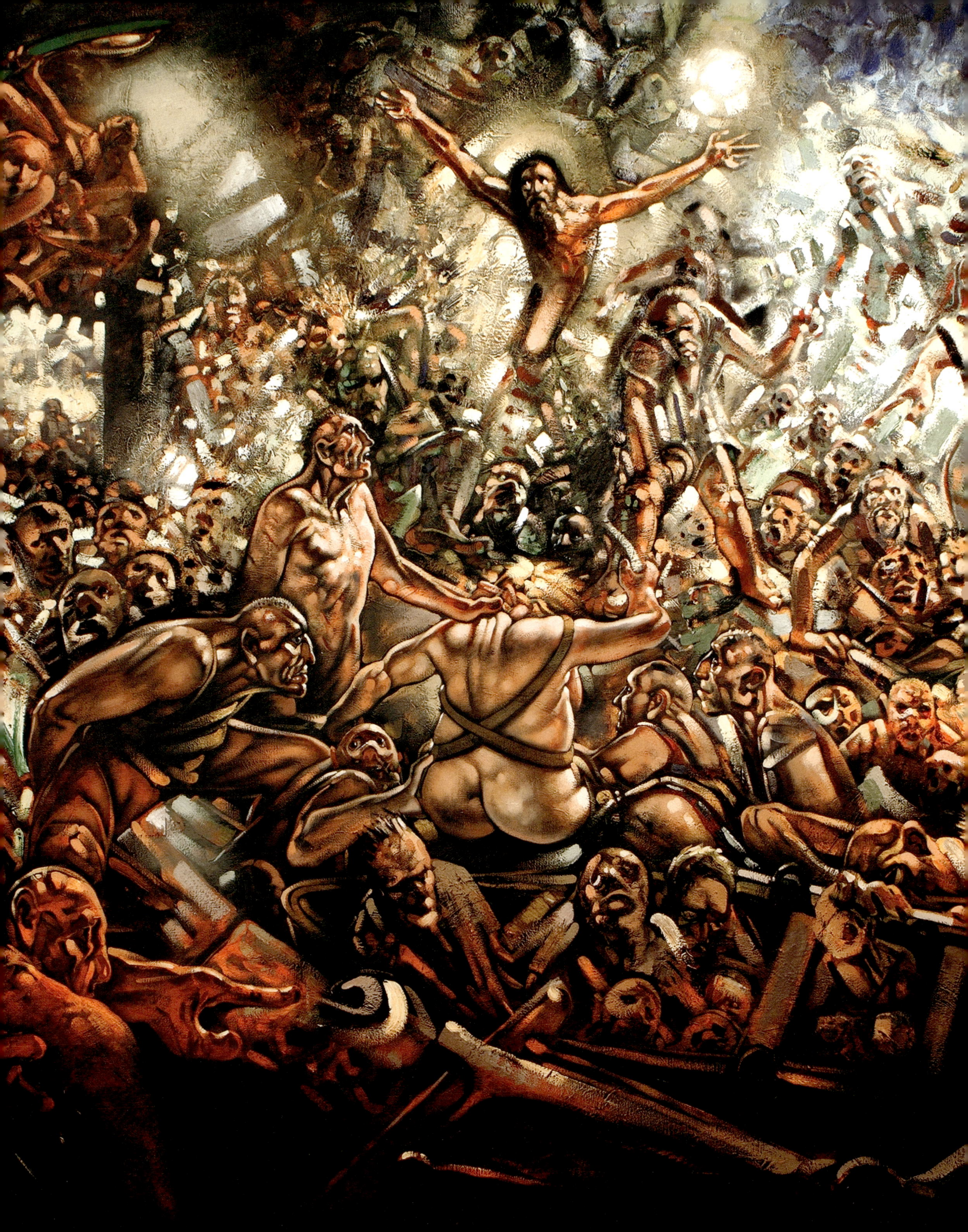

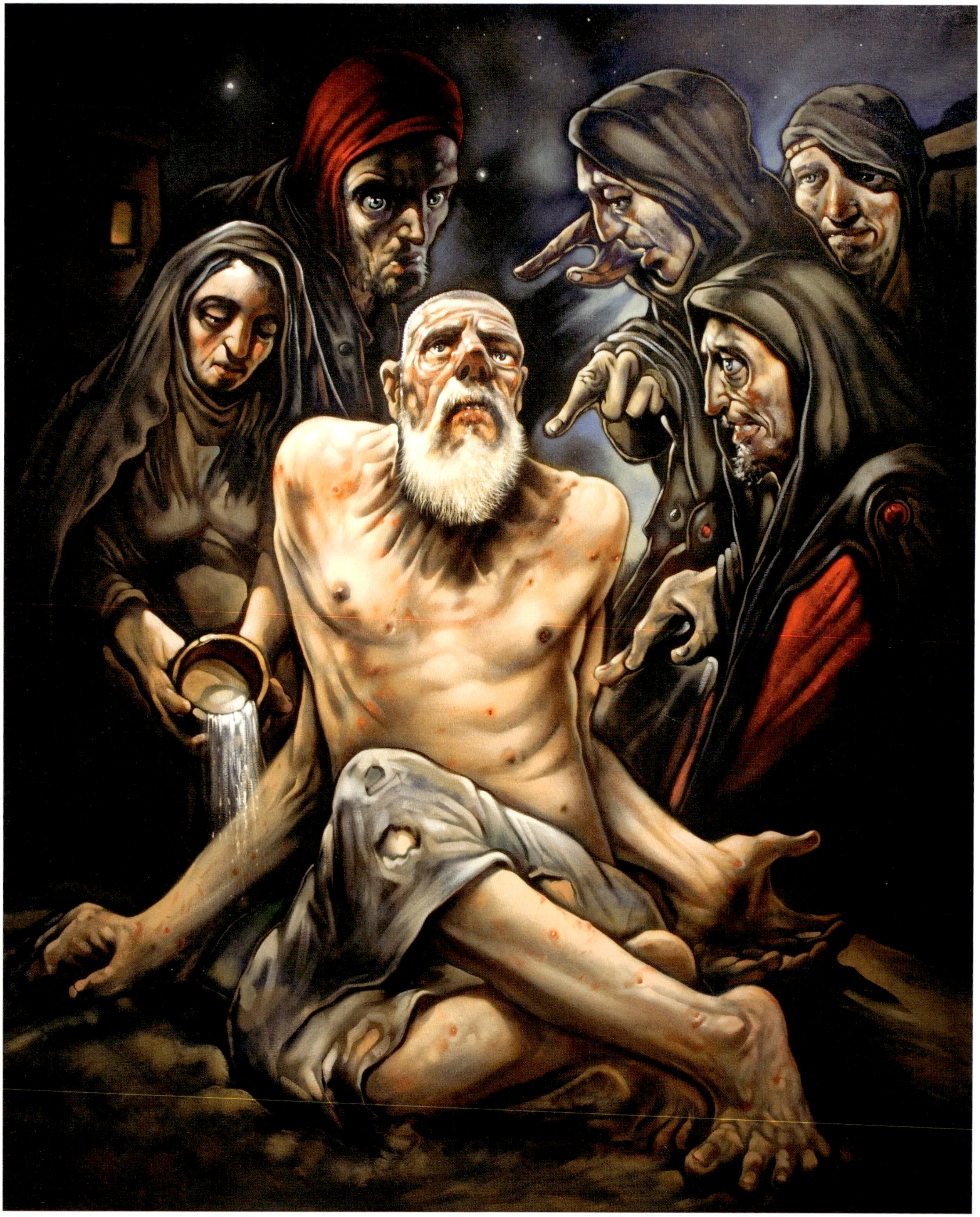

Job
2011 / oil on canvas / 182 x 152 cm
Alan and Karen Turner / photograph Antonio Parente

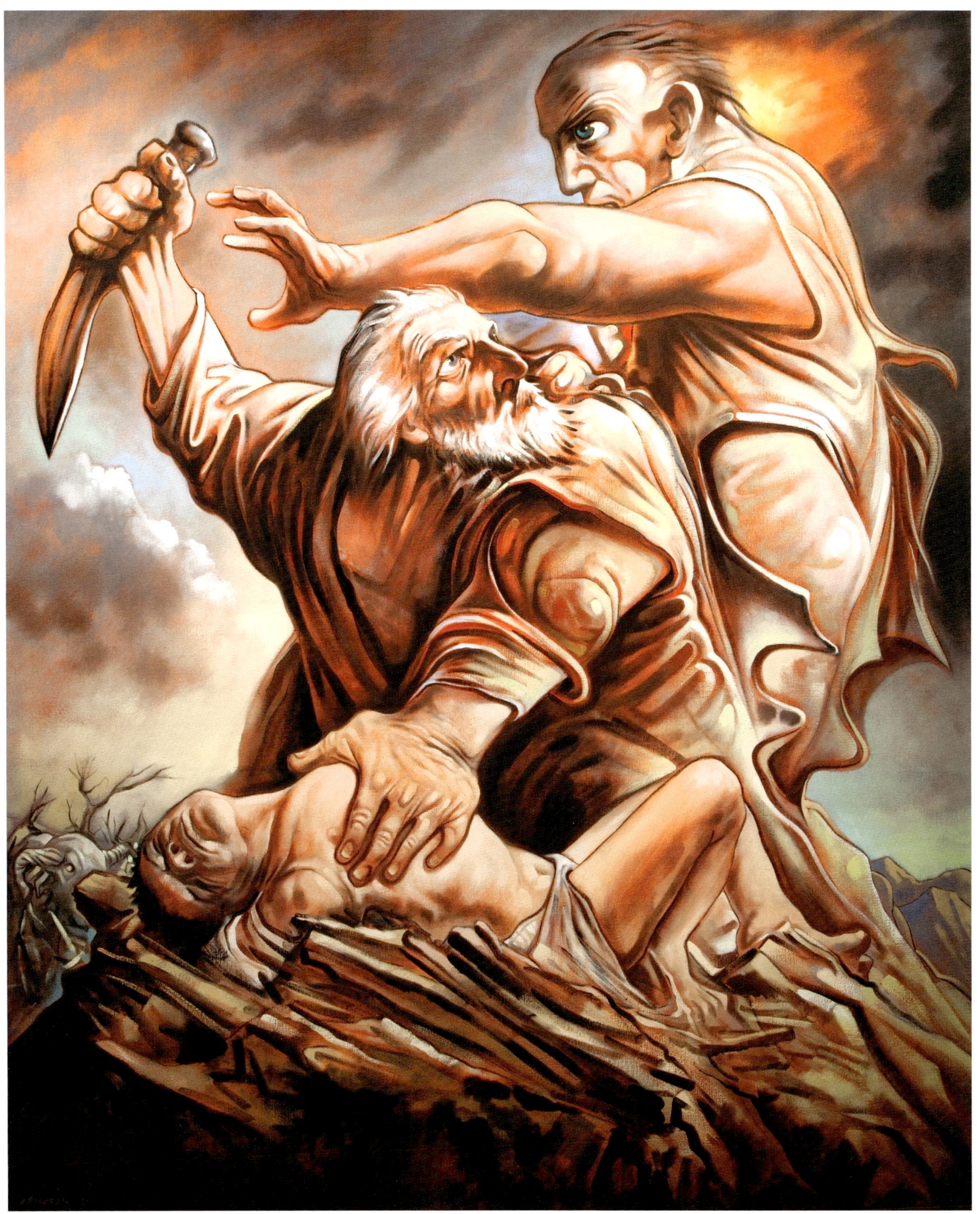

Abraham
2013 / oil on canvas / 182 x 152 cm
Alan and Karen Turner / photograph Antonio Parente

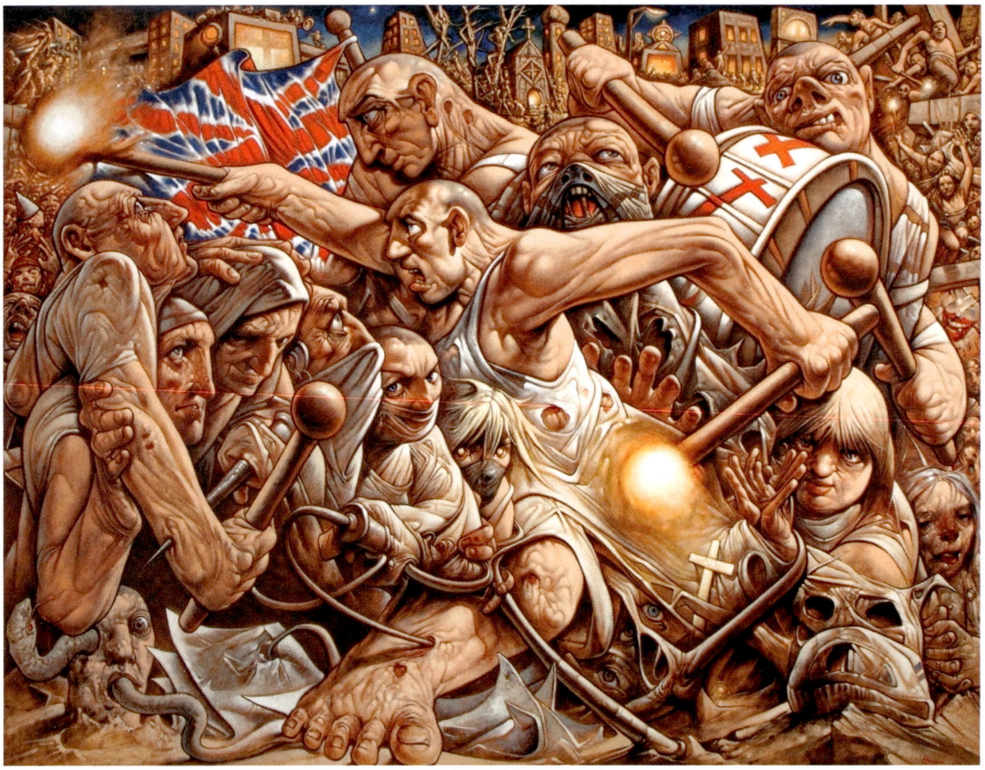

Babylon
2015 / oil on canvas / 183 x 244 cm
private collection, Switzerland / photograph Antonio Parente

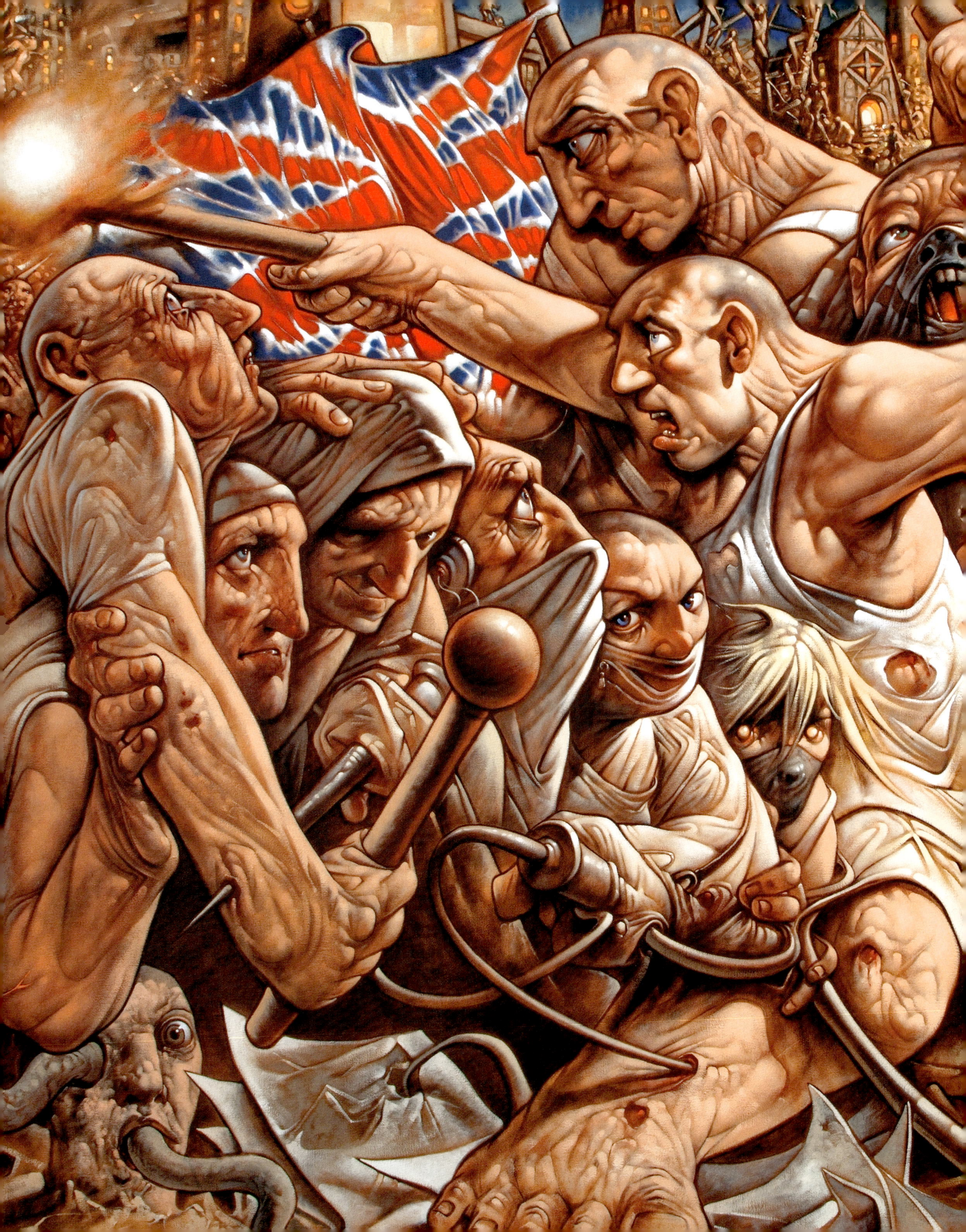

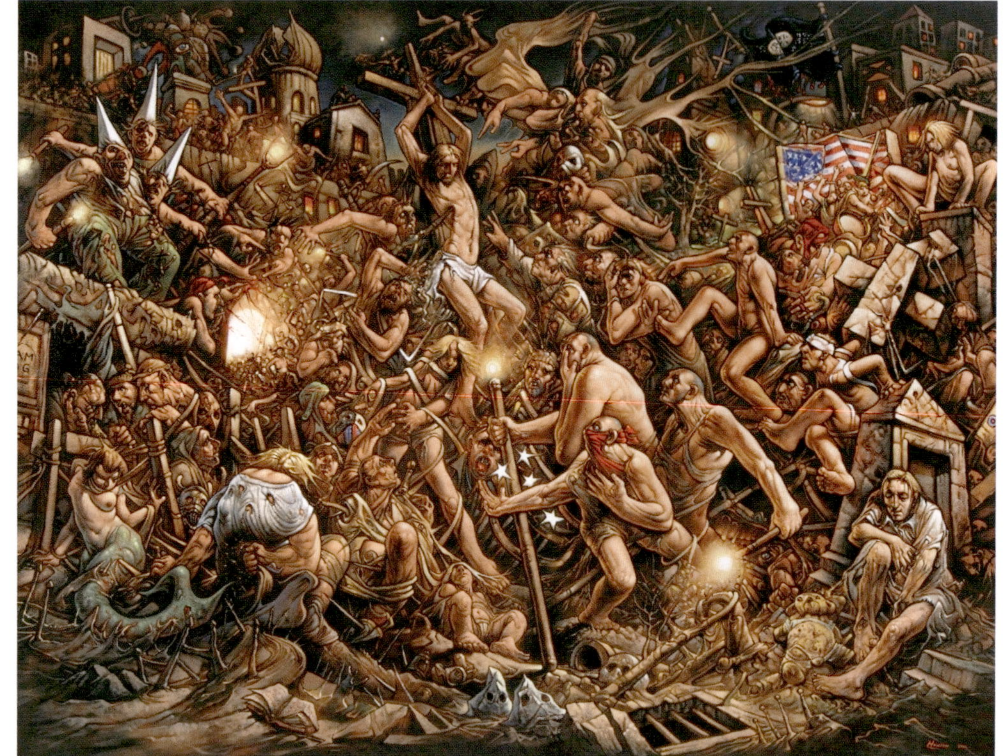

Prophecy
2016 / oil on canvas / 183.5 x 245 cm
private collection / photograph Antonio Parente

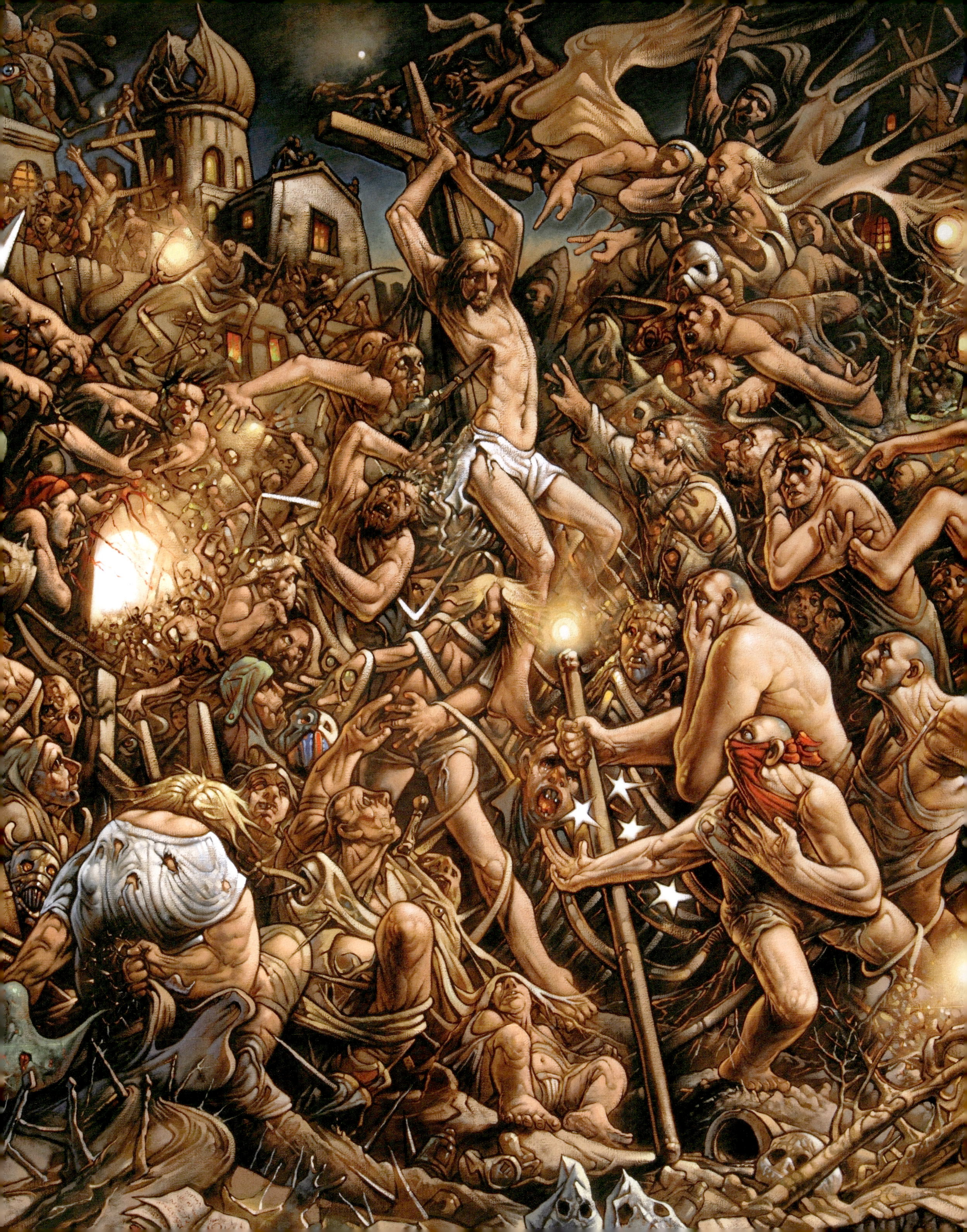

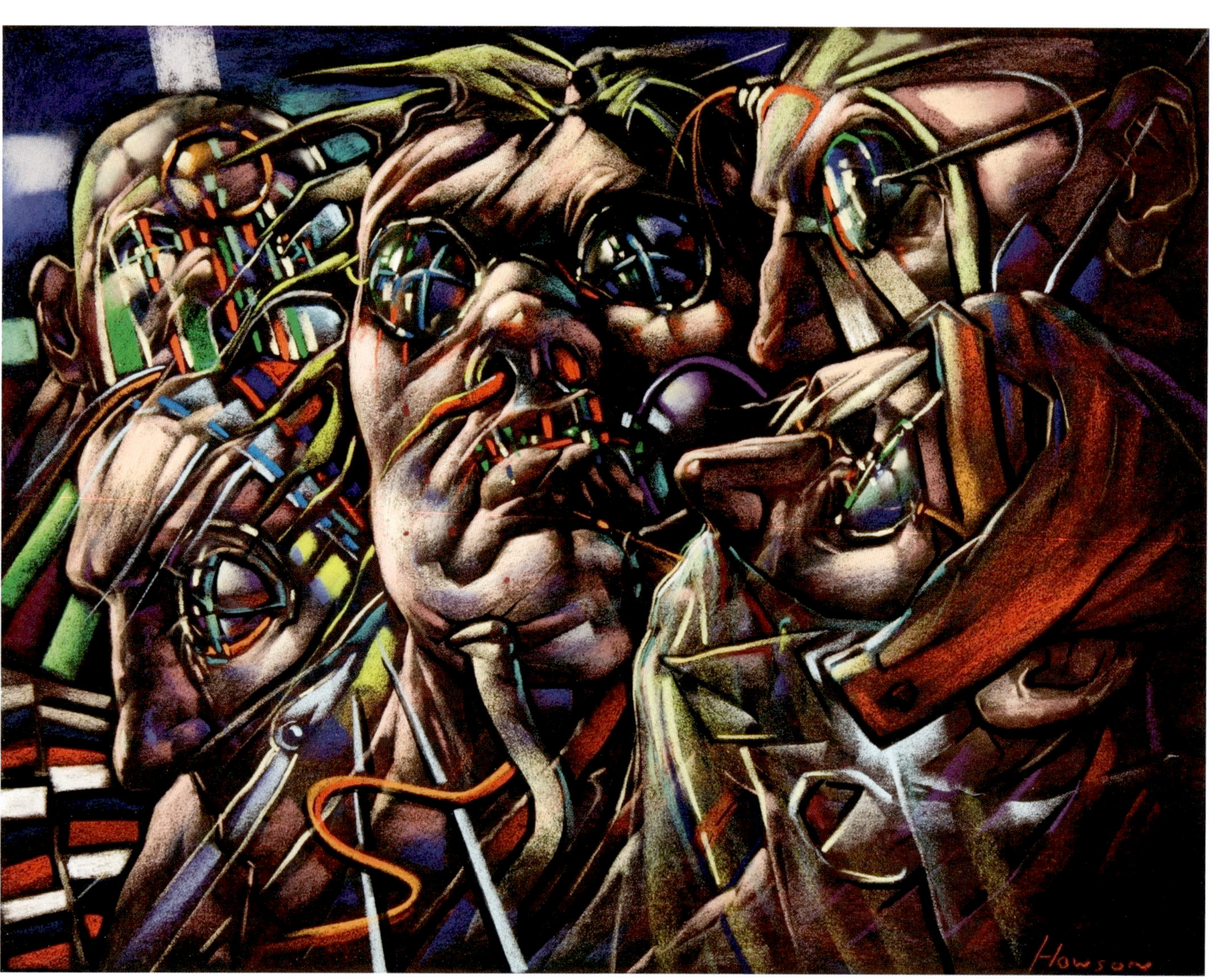

Raga and Contempt
2017 / pastel on paper / 49.5 x 64.5 cm
private collection, Switzerland / photograph Antonio Parente

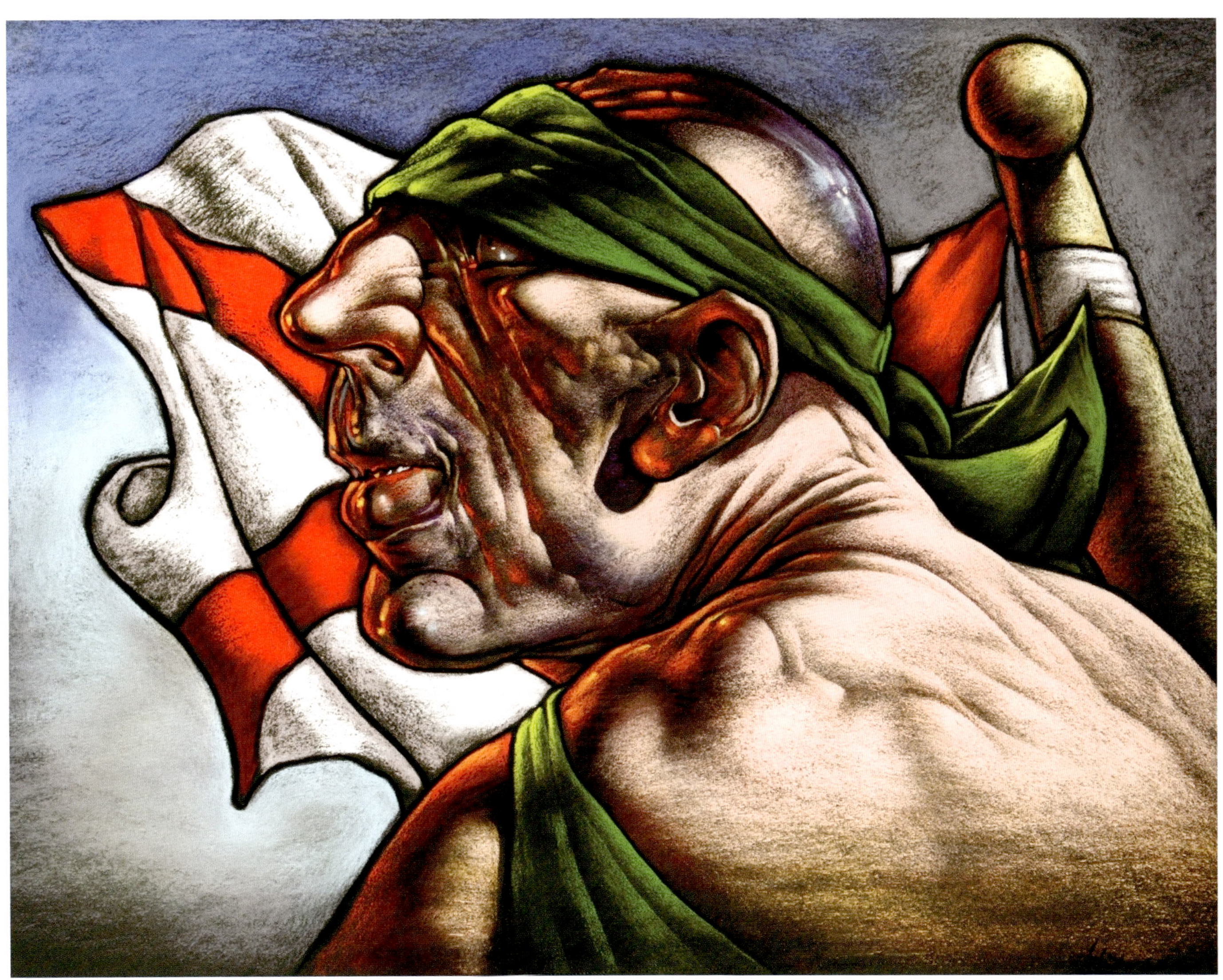

Barbarian
2017 / pastel on paper / 49.5 x 64.5 cm
private collection, Switzerland / photograph Antonio Parente

Christ Surrounded by His Disciples When He Meets Thomas
2019 / oil on canvas / 182 x 152 cm
Alan and Karen Turner / photograph Antonio Parente

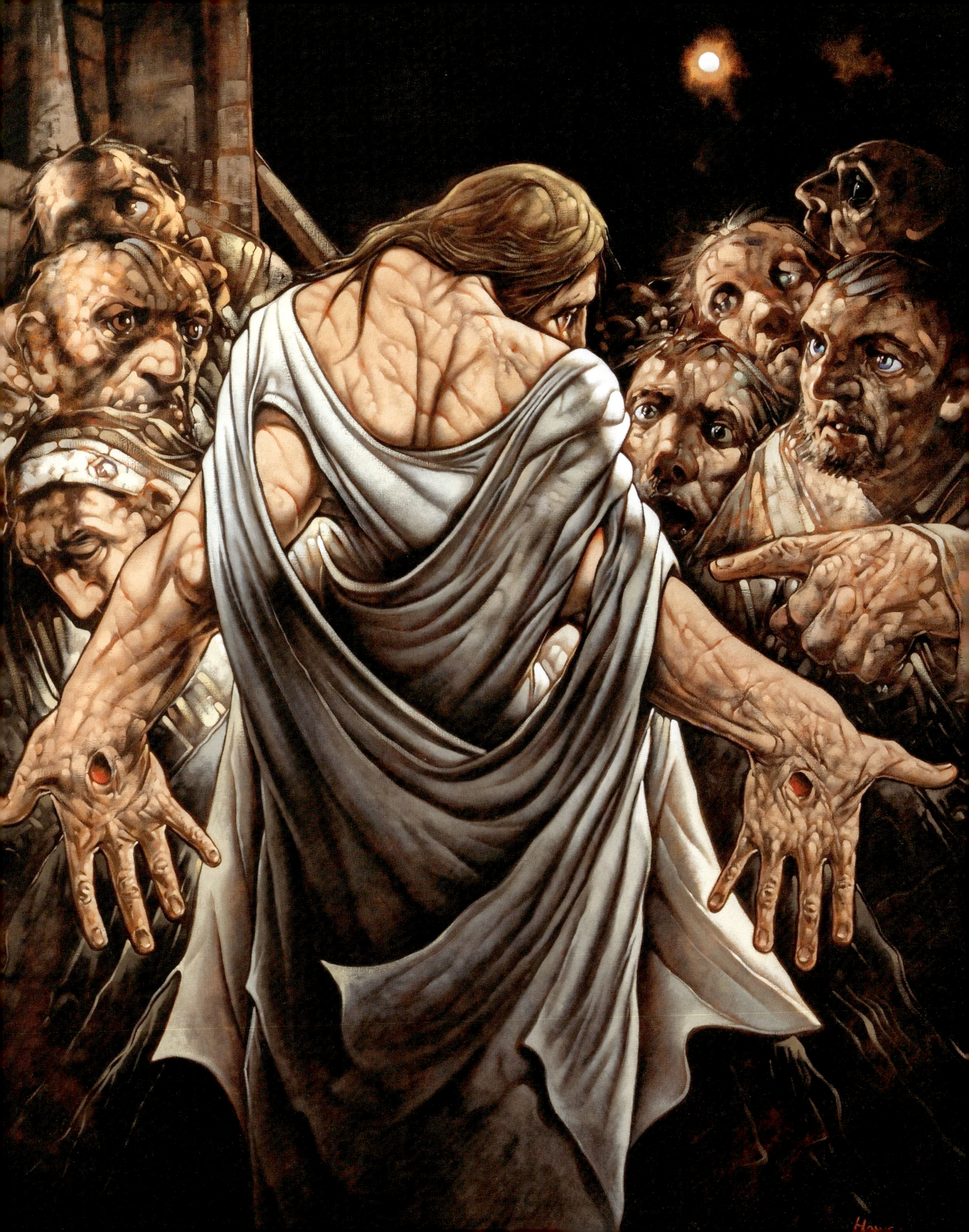

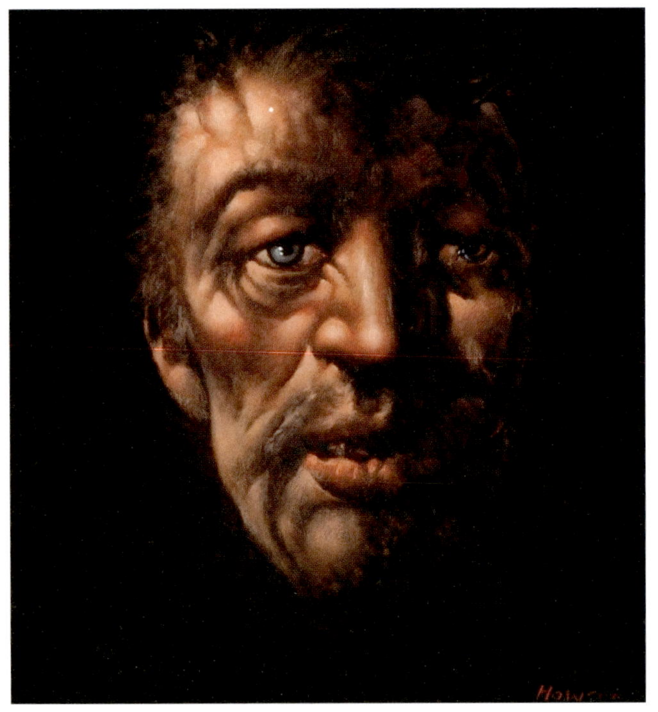

Apostles I–XII
Thomas
2019 / oil on gessoed panel / 22 x 21 cm
John J. Studzinski CBE / photograph Ian Marshall

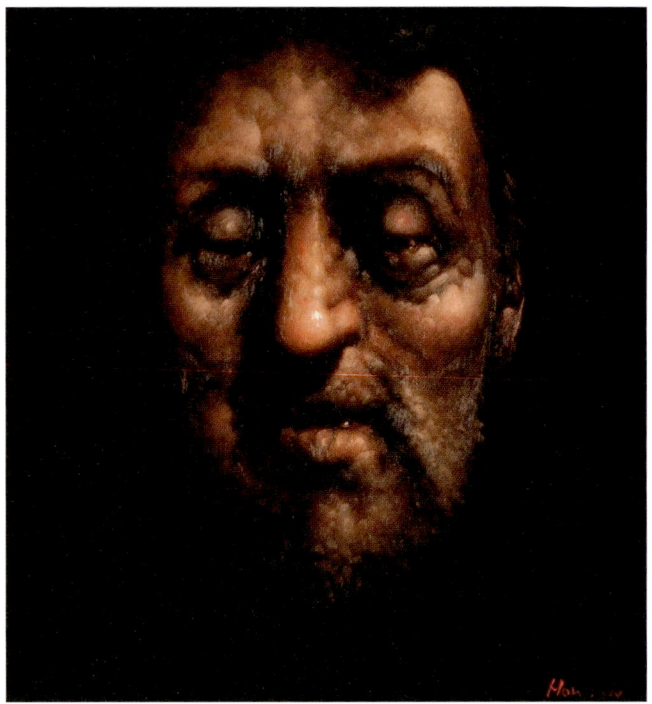

Apostles I–XII
Thaddeus
2019 / oil on gessoed panel / 22 x 21 cm
John J. Studzinski CBE / photograph Ian Marshall

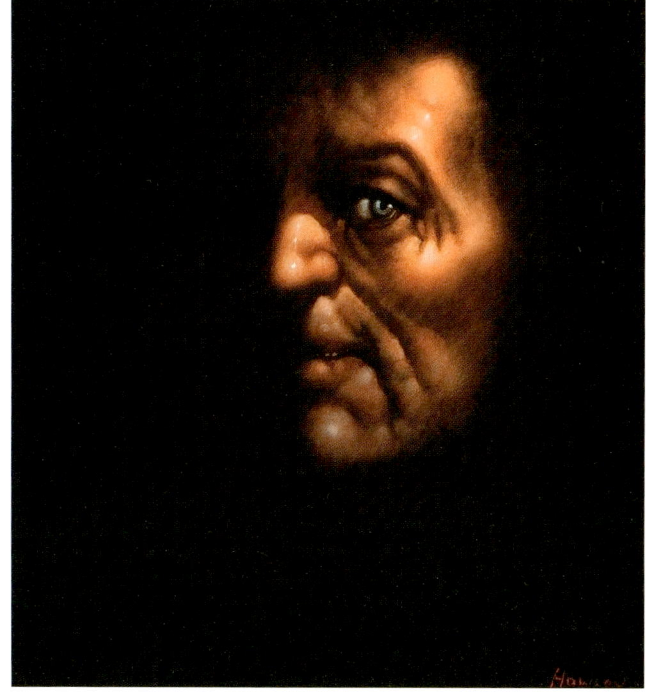

Apostles I–XII
Simon
2019 / oil on gessoed panel / 22 x 21 cm
John J. Studzinski CBE / photograph Ian Marshall

Apostles I–XII
Matthias
2019 / oil on gessoed panel / 22 x 21 cm
John J. Studzinski CBE / photograph Ian Marshall

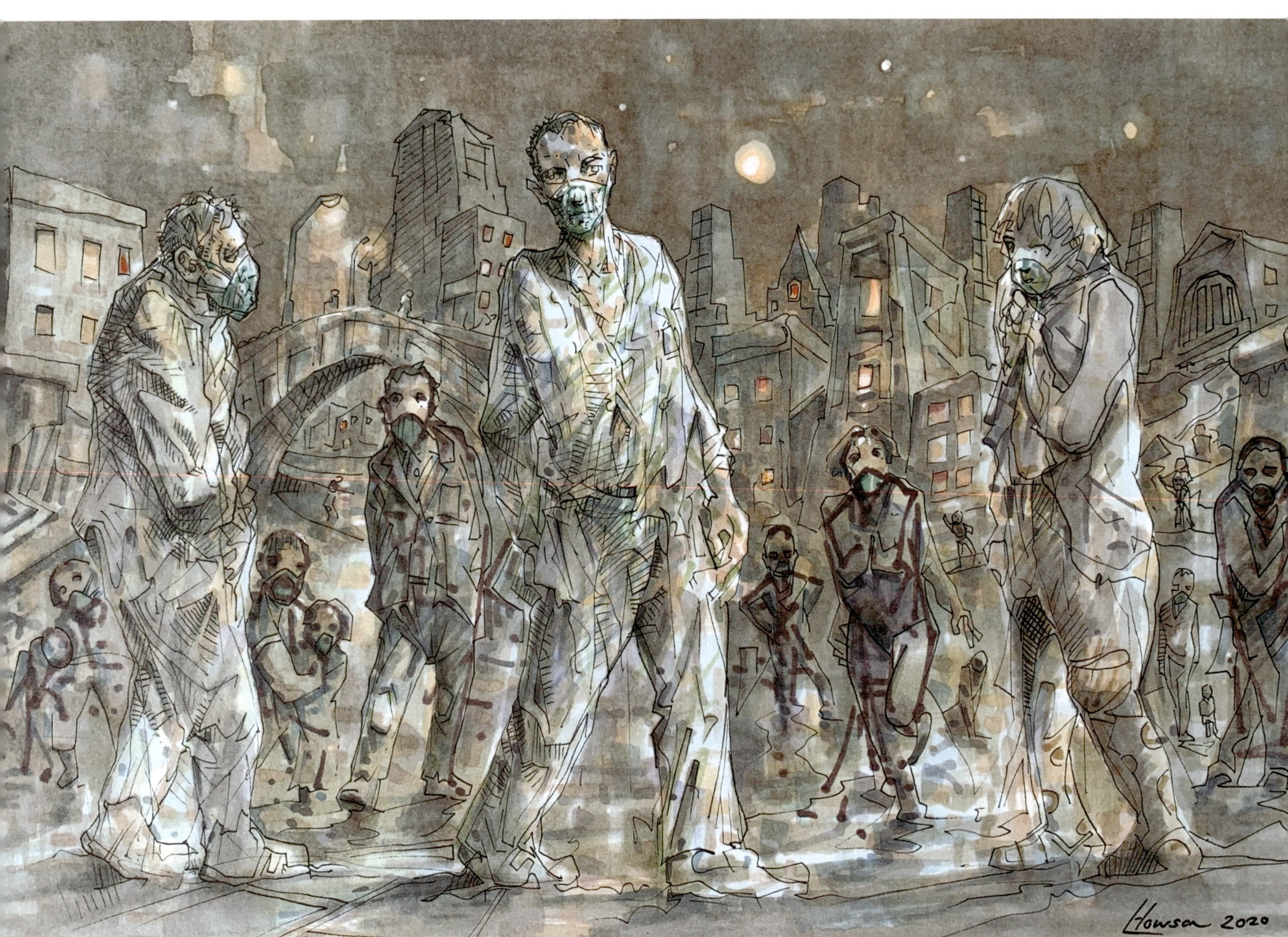

An Important Announcement
2020 / inks on paper / 20.5 x 30.5 cm
private collection / photograph Antonio Parente

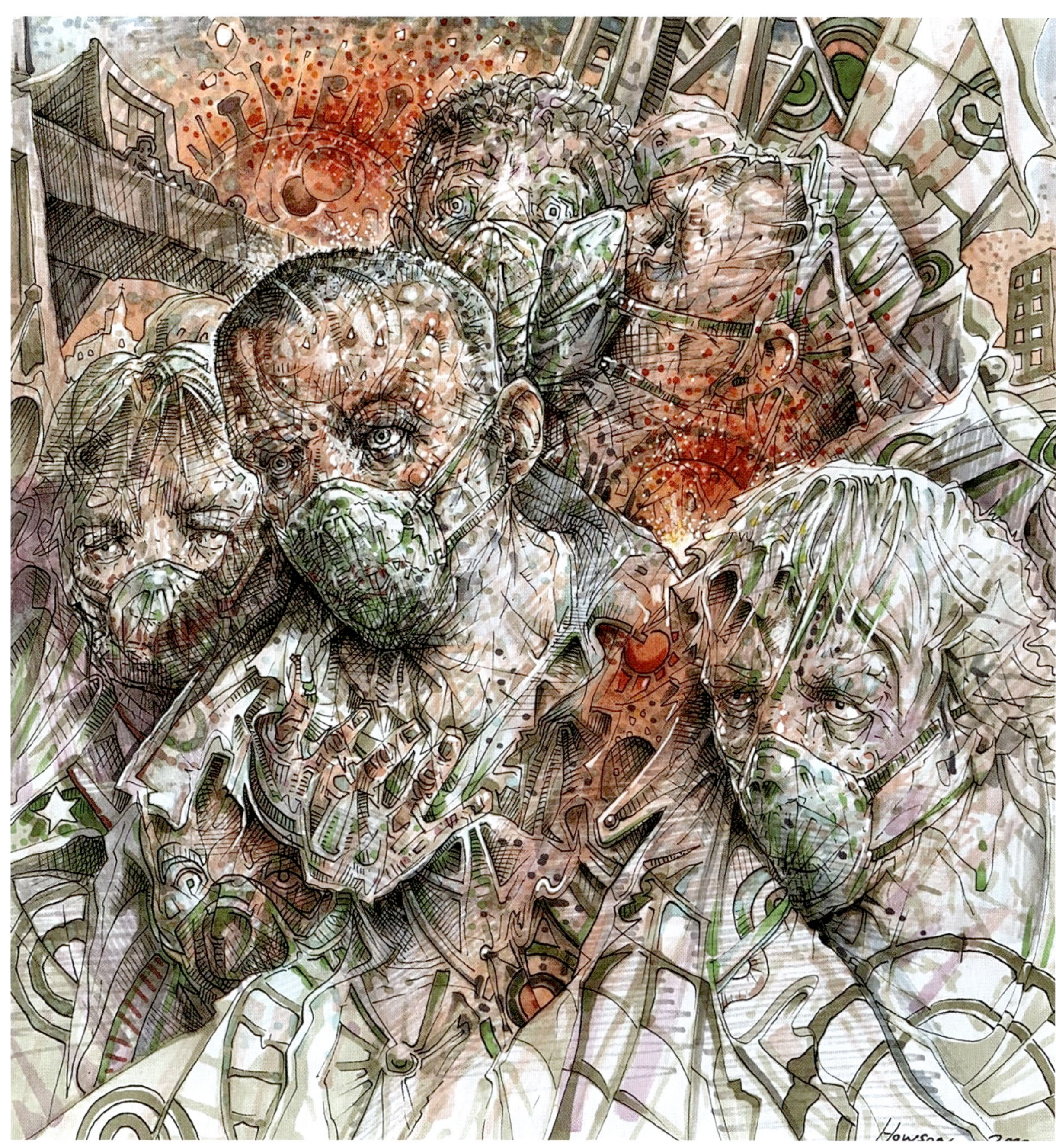

Thursday at Eight
2020 / inks on paper / 24 x 23 cm
private collection / photograph Antonio Parente

Jupiter Tonans
2020 / oil on canvas / 183 x 153 cm
Flowers Gallery / photograph Antonio Parente

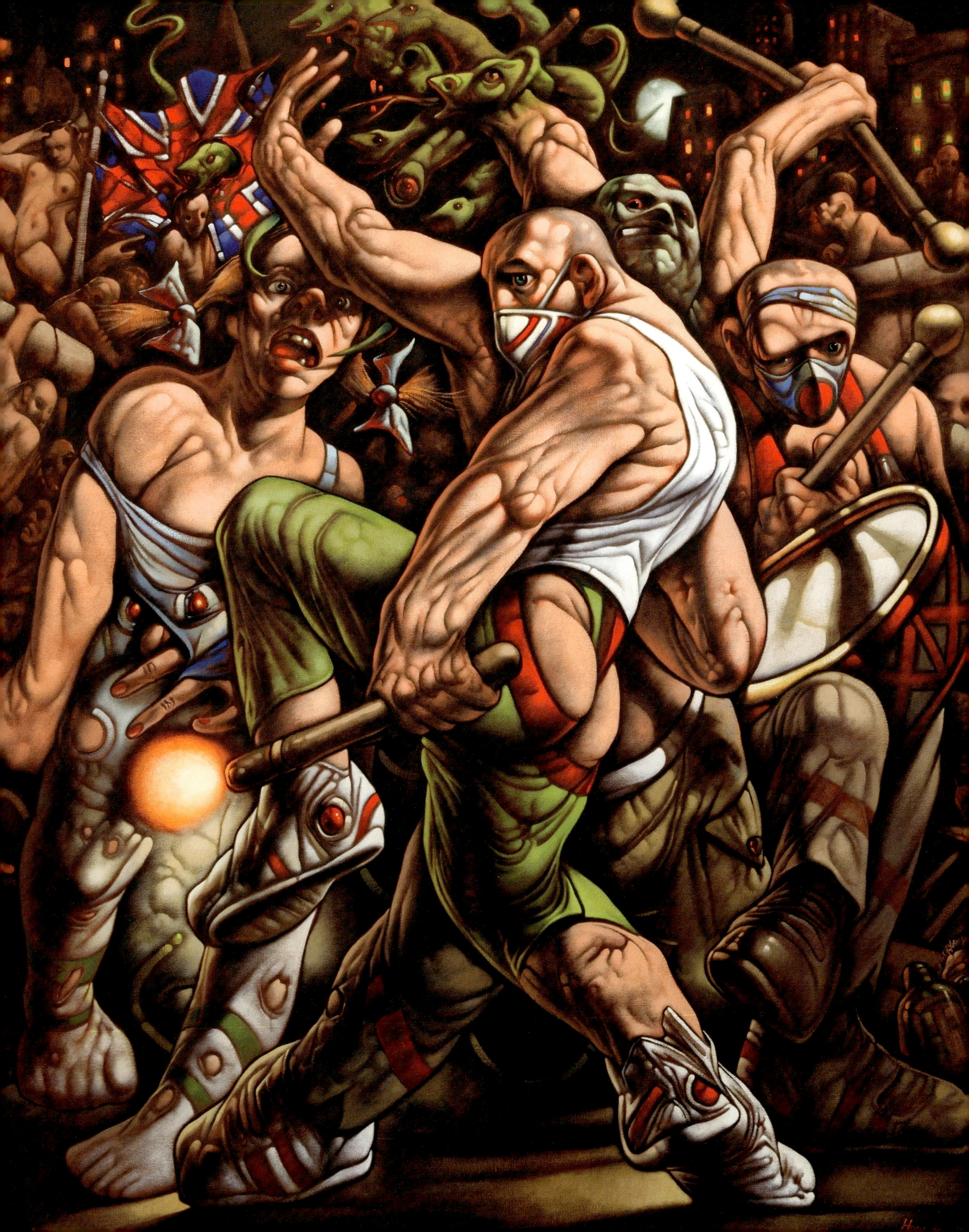

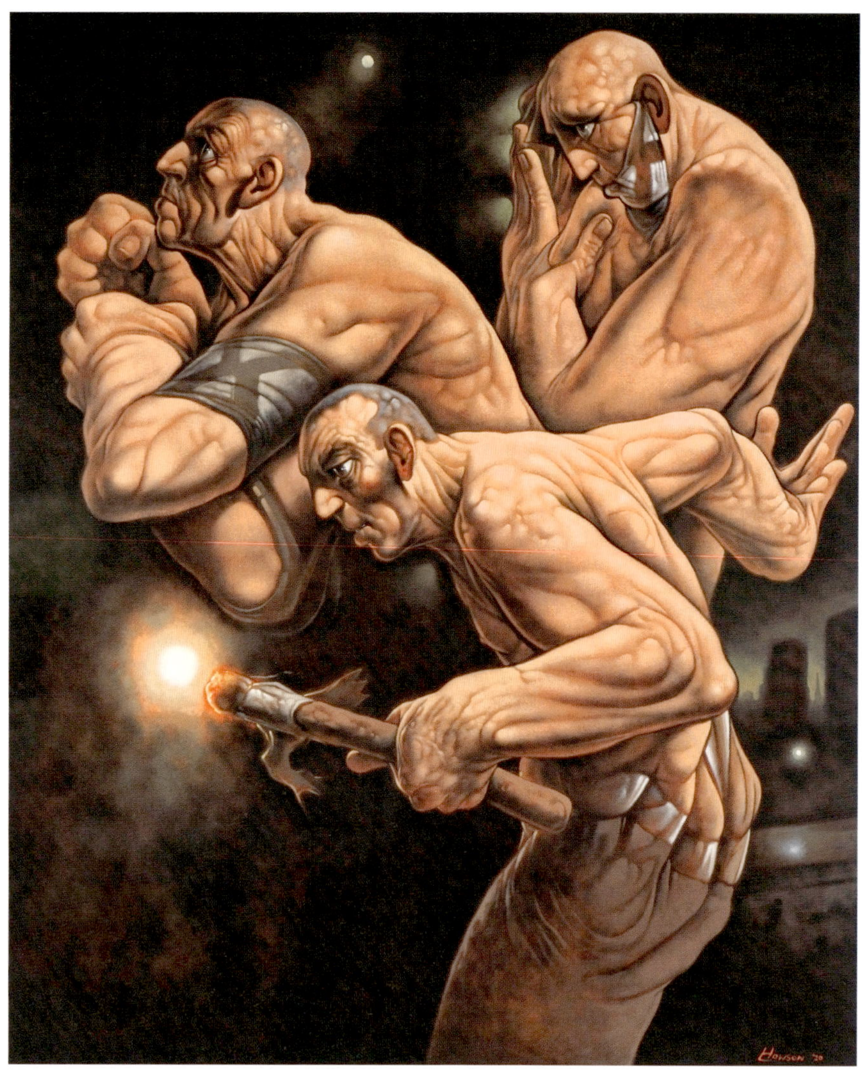

Trinity
2020 / oil on canvas / 183 x 153 cm
Flowers Gallery / photograph Antonio Parente

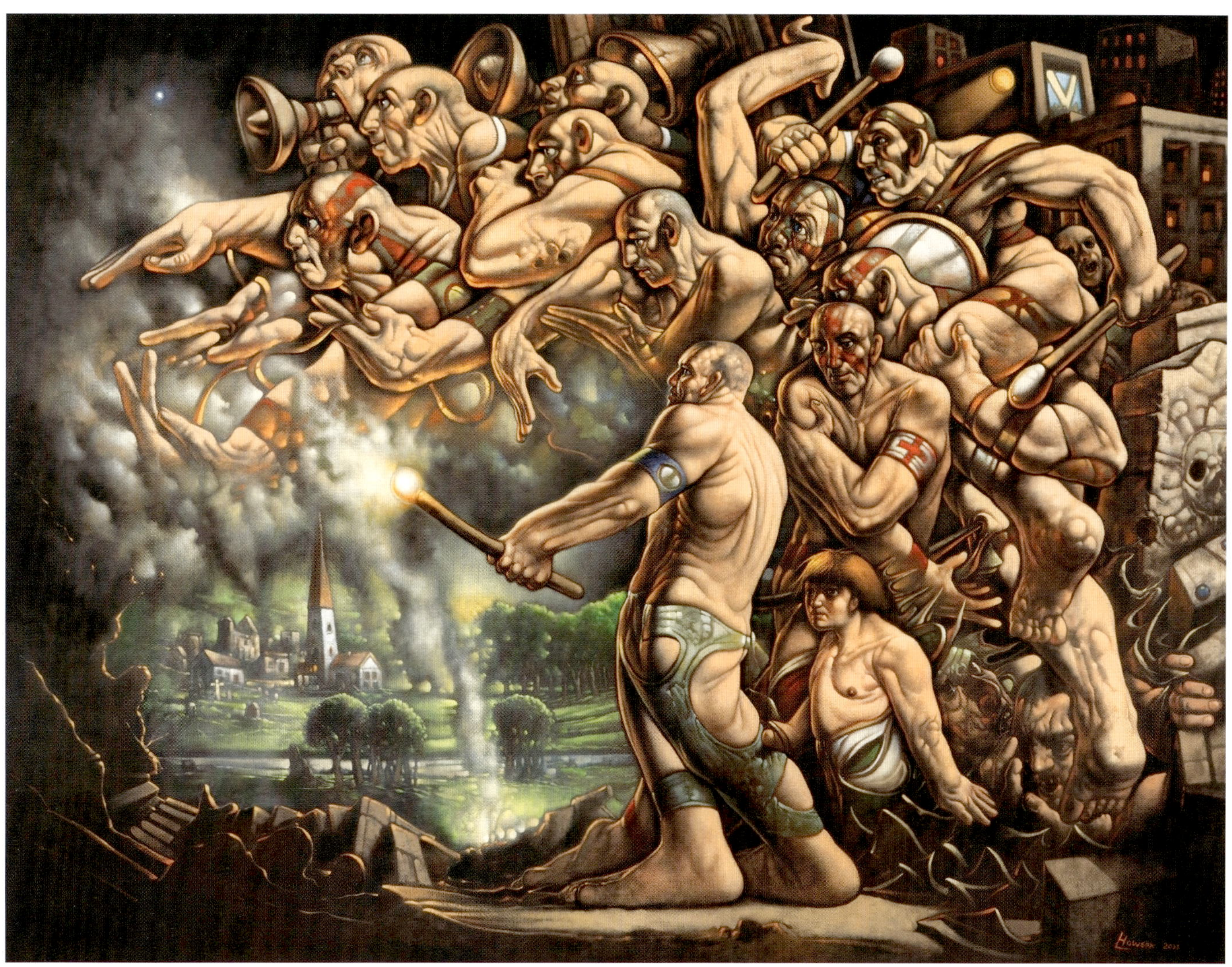

Popolo Minuto
2021 / oil on canvas / 183 x 244.5cm
private collection, Switzerland / photograph Antonio Parente

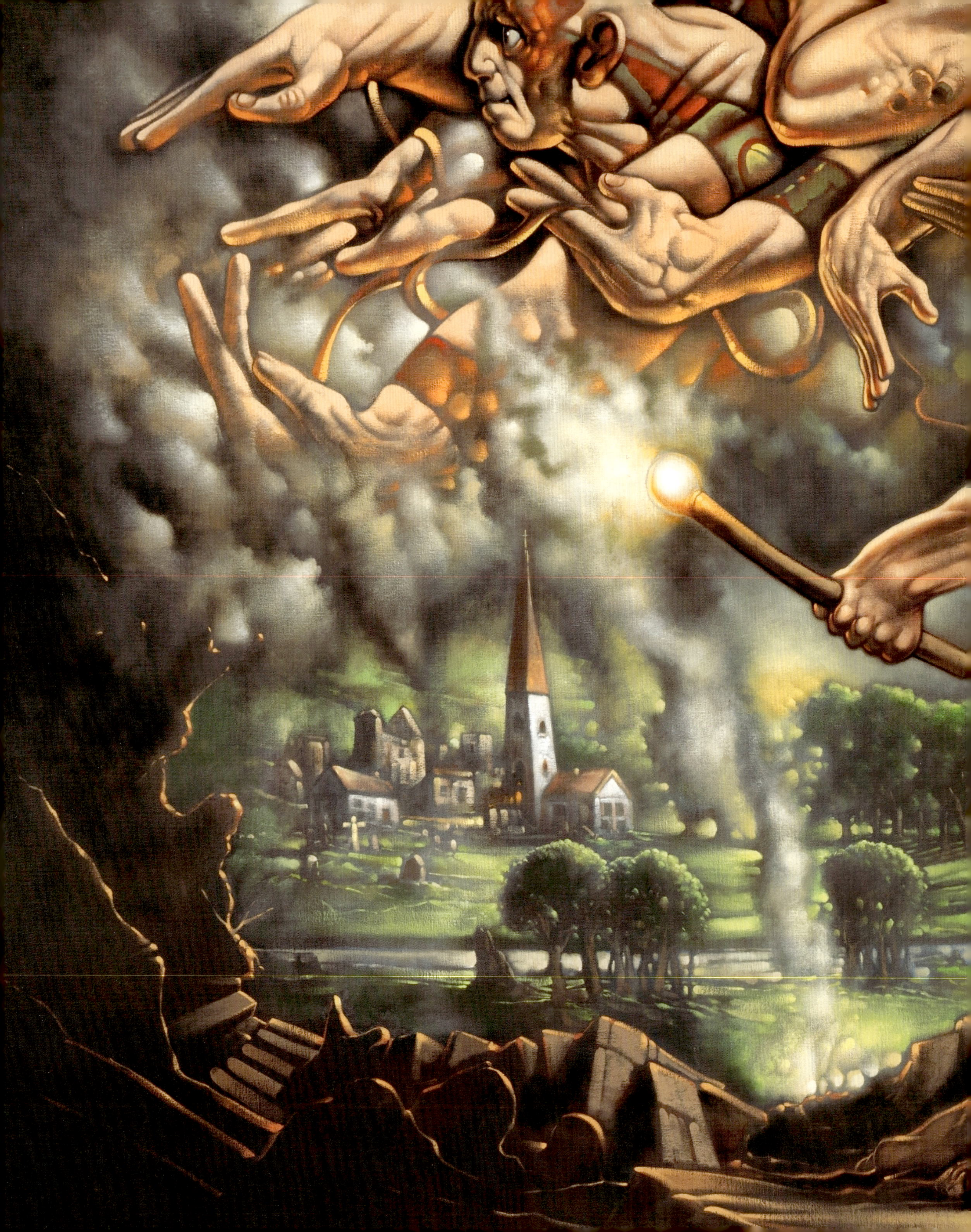

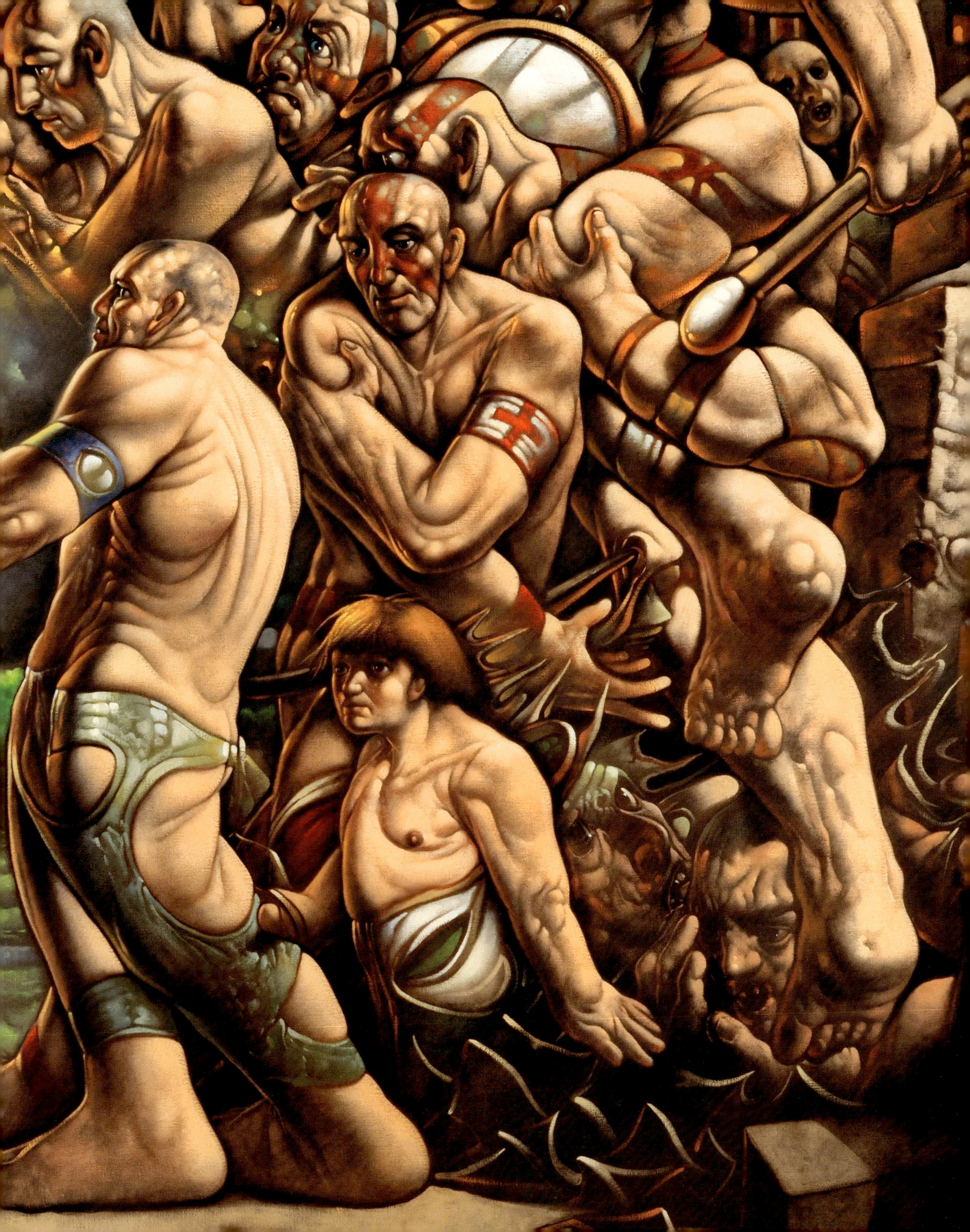

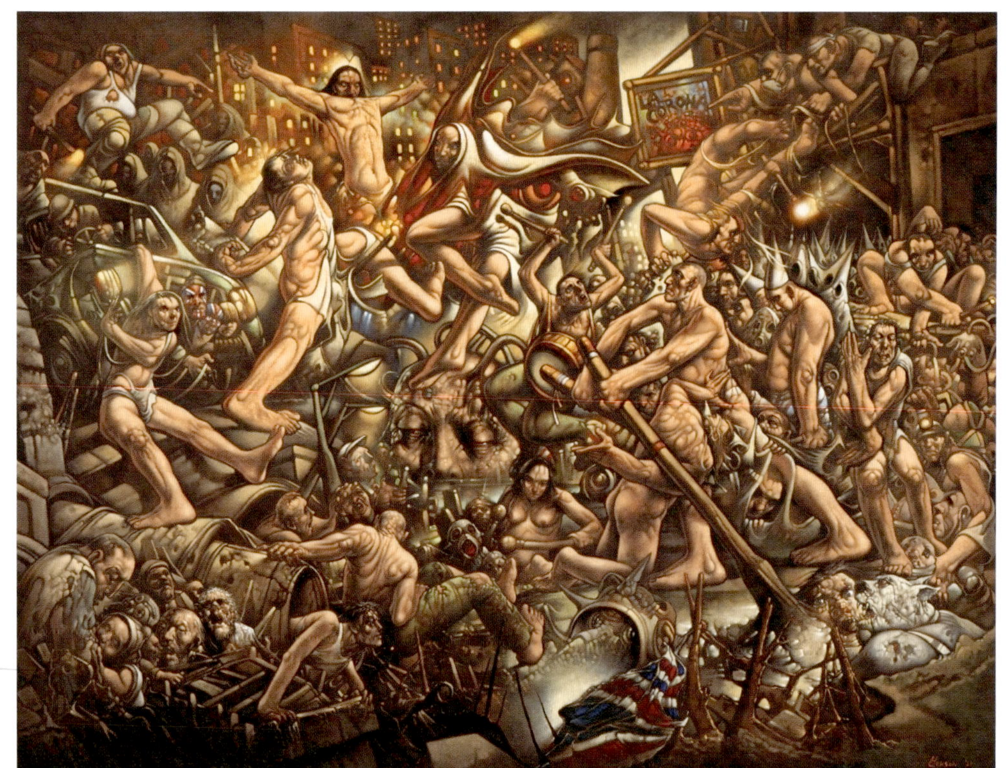

Phlegethon
2021 / oil on canvas / 183 x 244 cm
private collection / photograph Antonio Parente

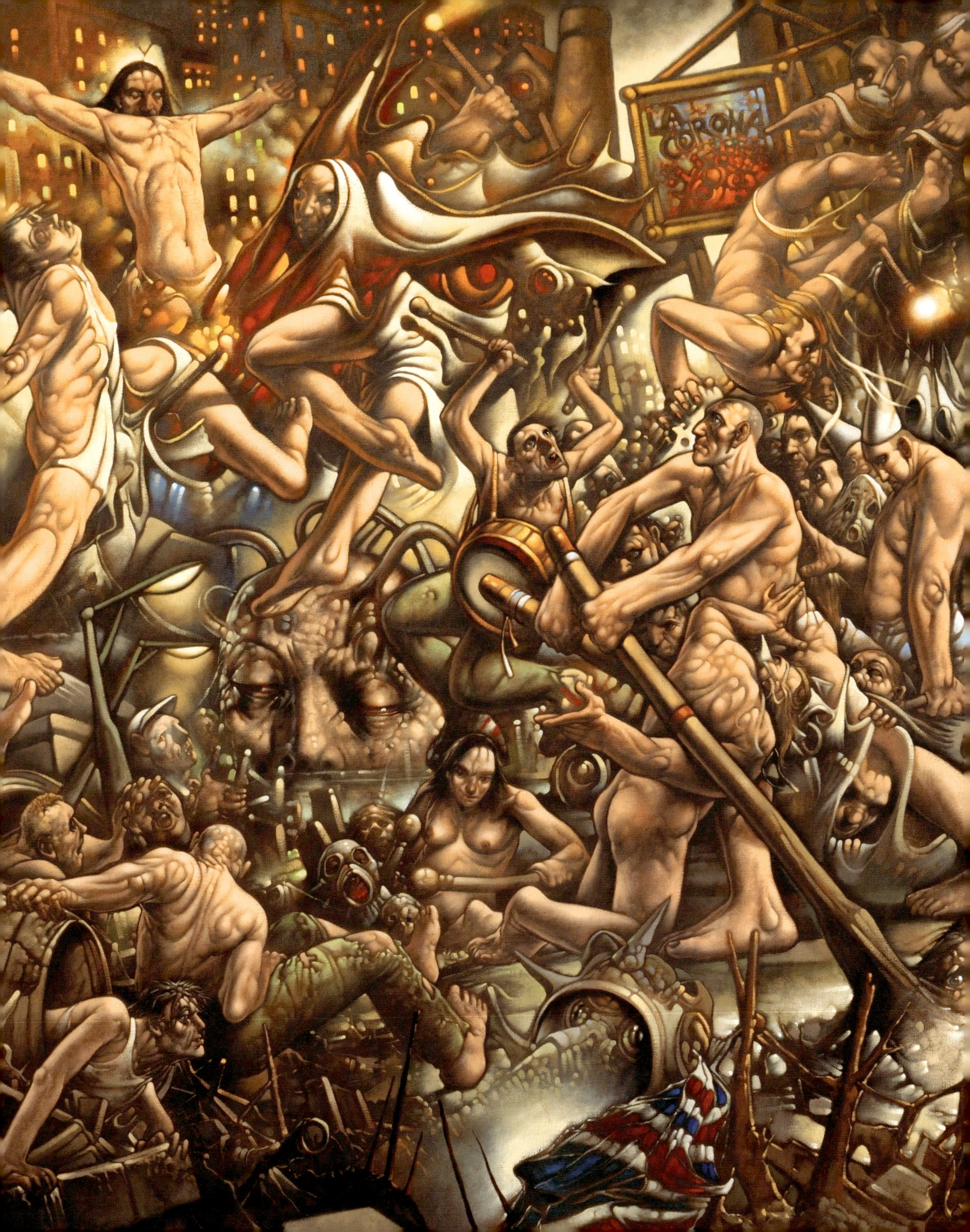

LA CORONA

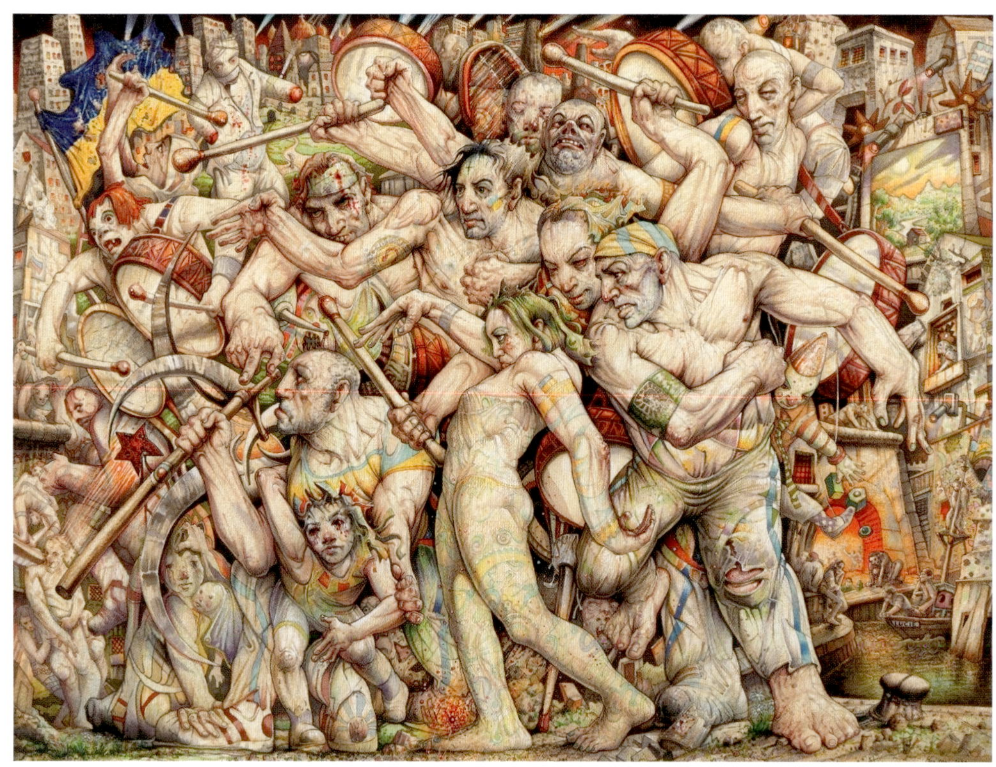

Veritas Numquam Perit (Truth Never Perishes)
2022 / inks on paper / 51 x 76 cm
Flowers Gallery / photograph Antonio Parente

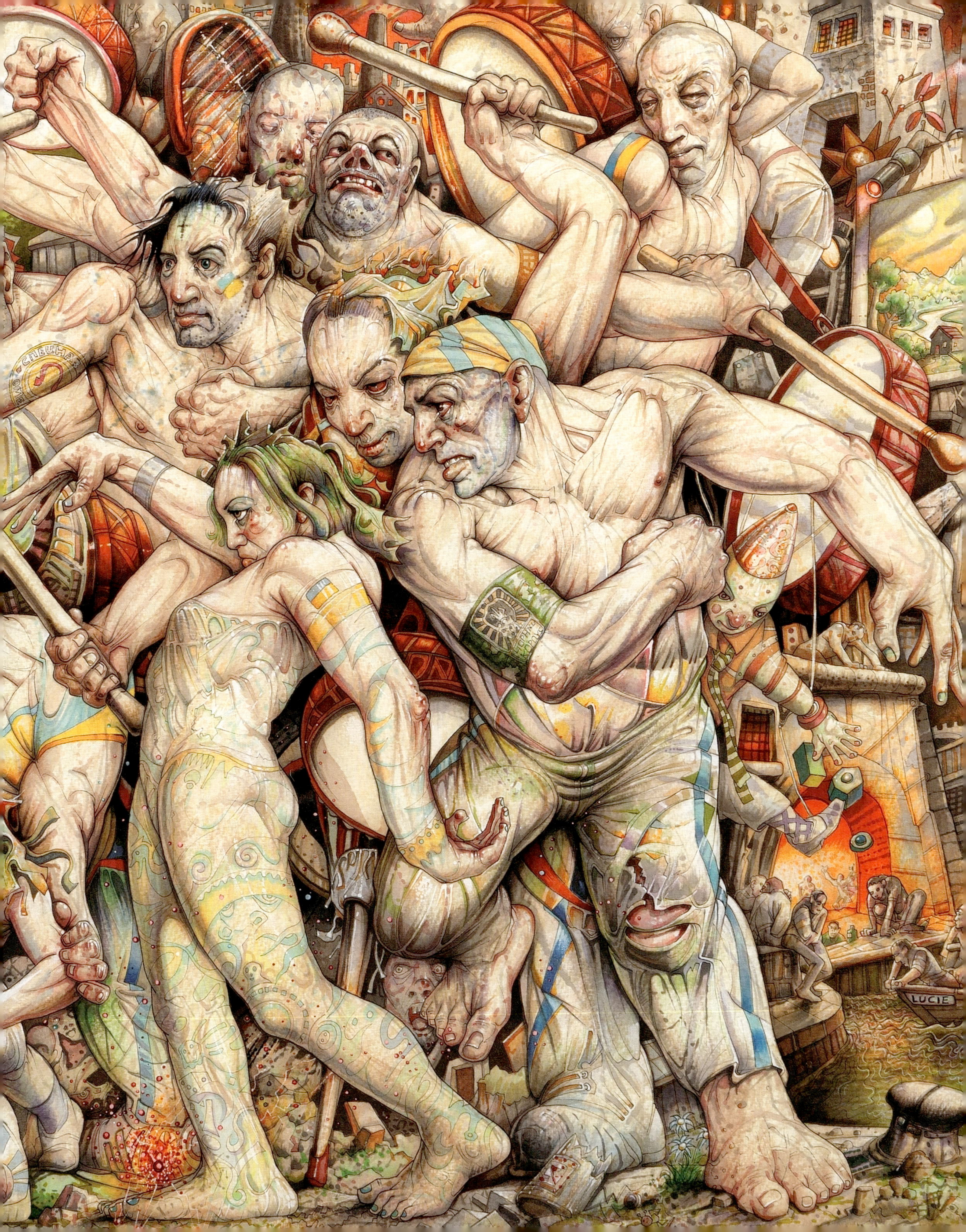
СПЕЦНАЗ
LUCIE

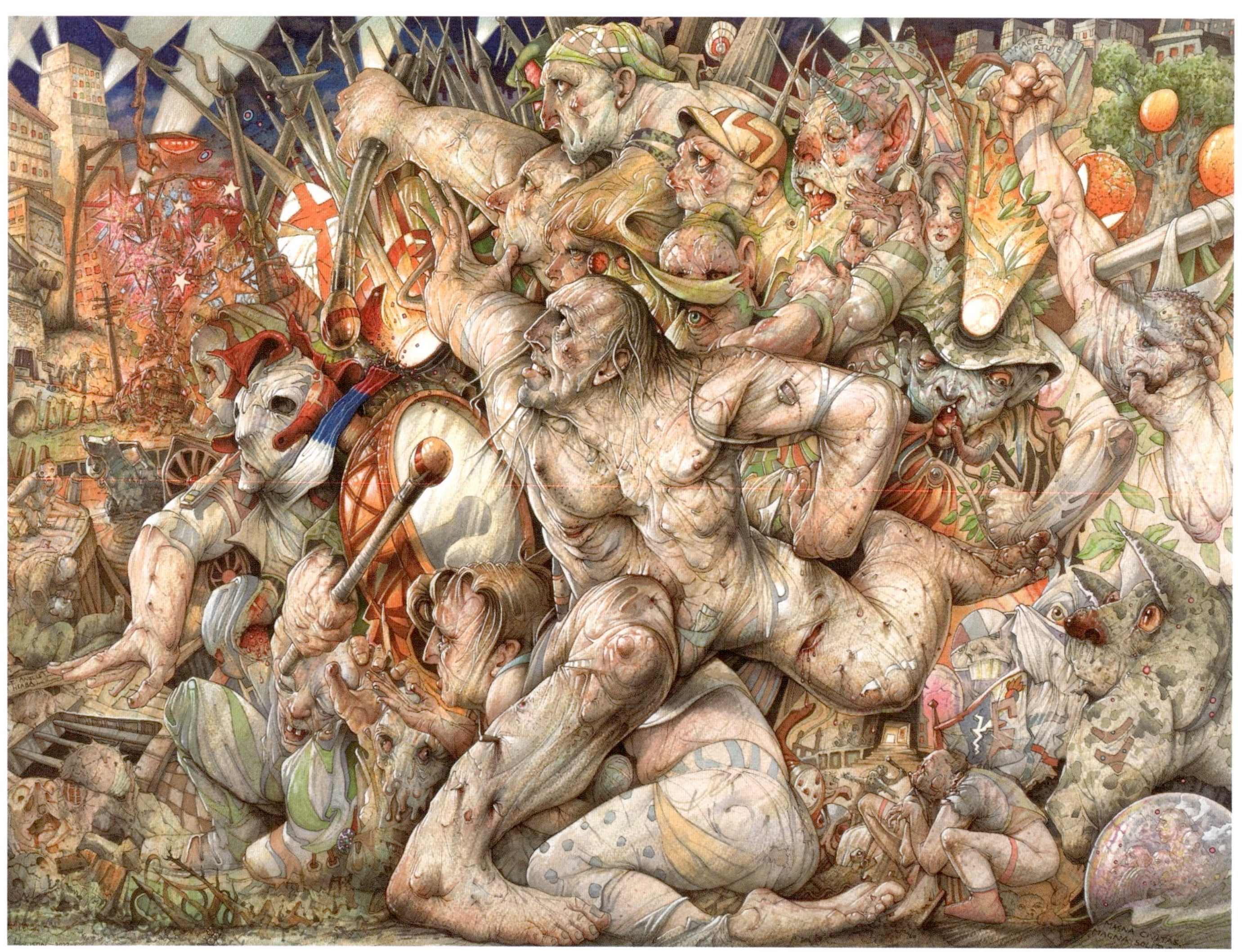

Iuppeter Tonans (Jupiter the Thunderer)
2022 / inks on paper / 51 x 76 cm
private collection / photograph Ian Marshall

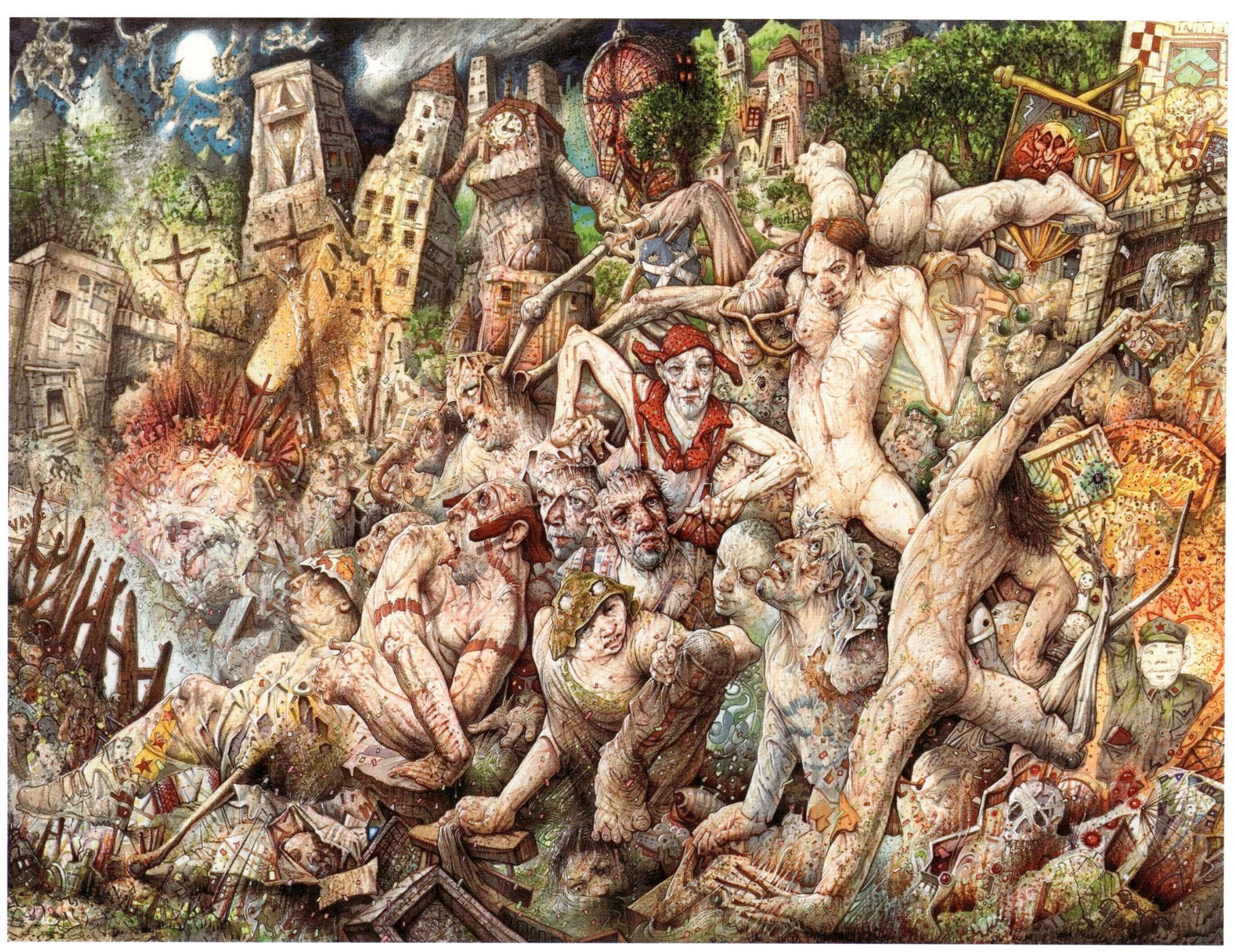

What Can't Be Cured Must Be Endured
2021 / ink on paper / 51 x 76 cm
private collection / photograph Ian Marshall

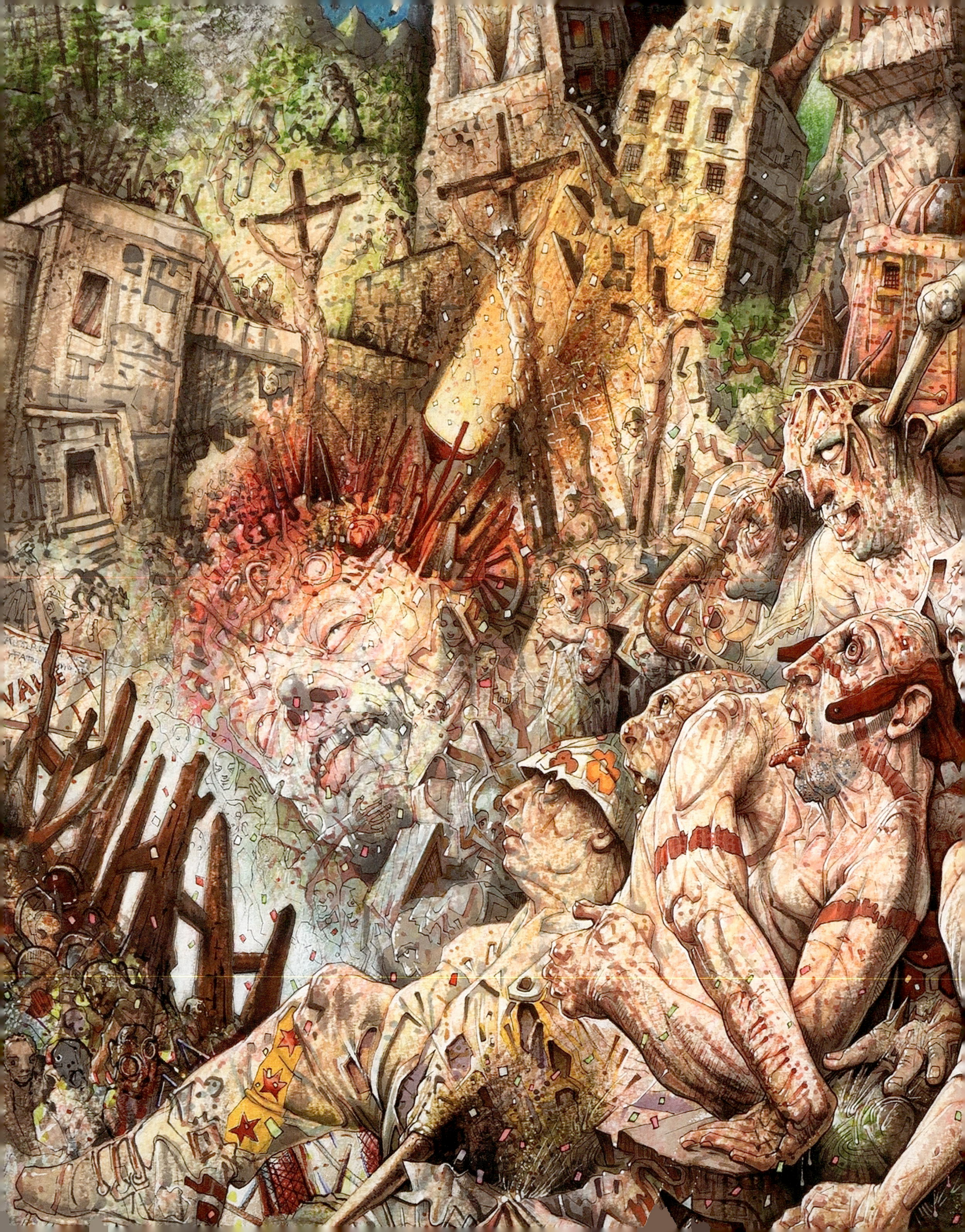

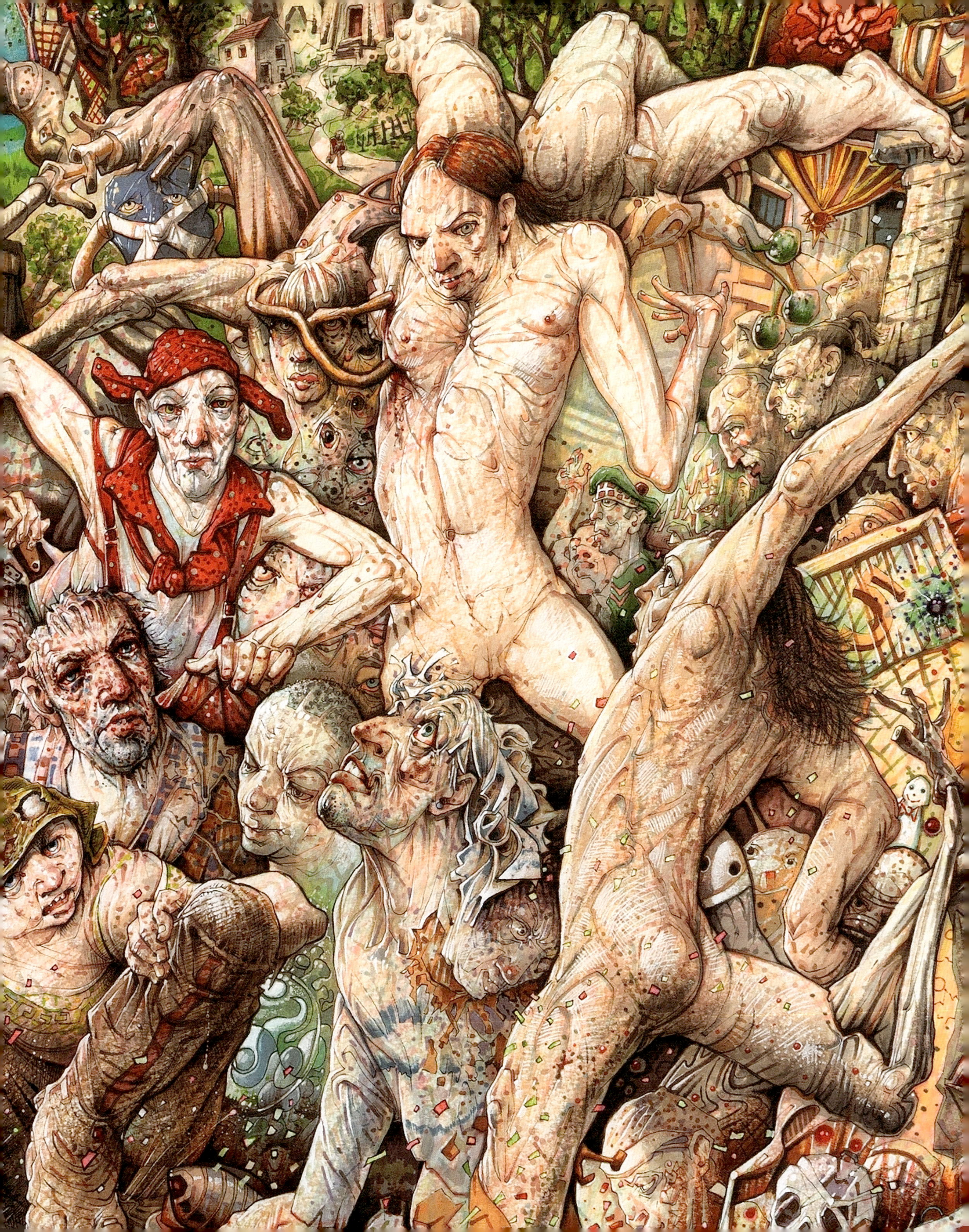

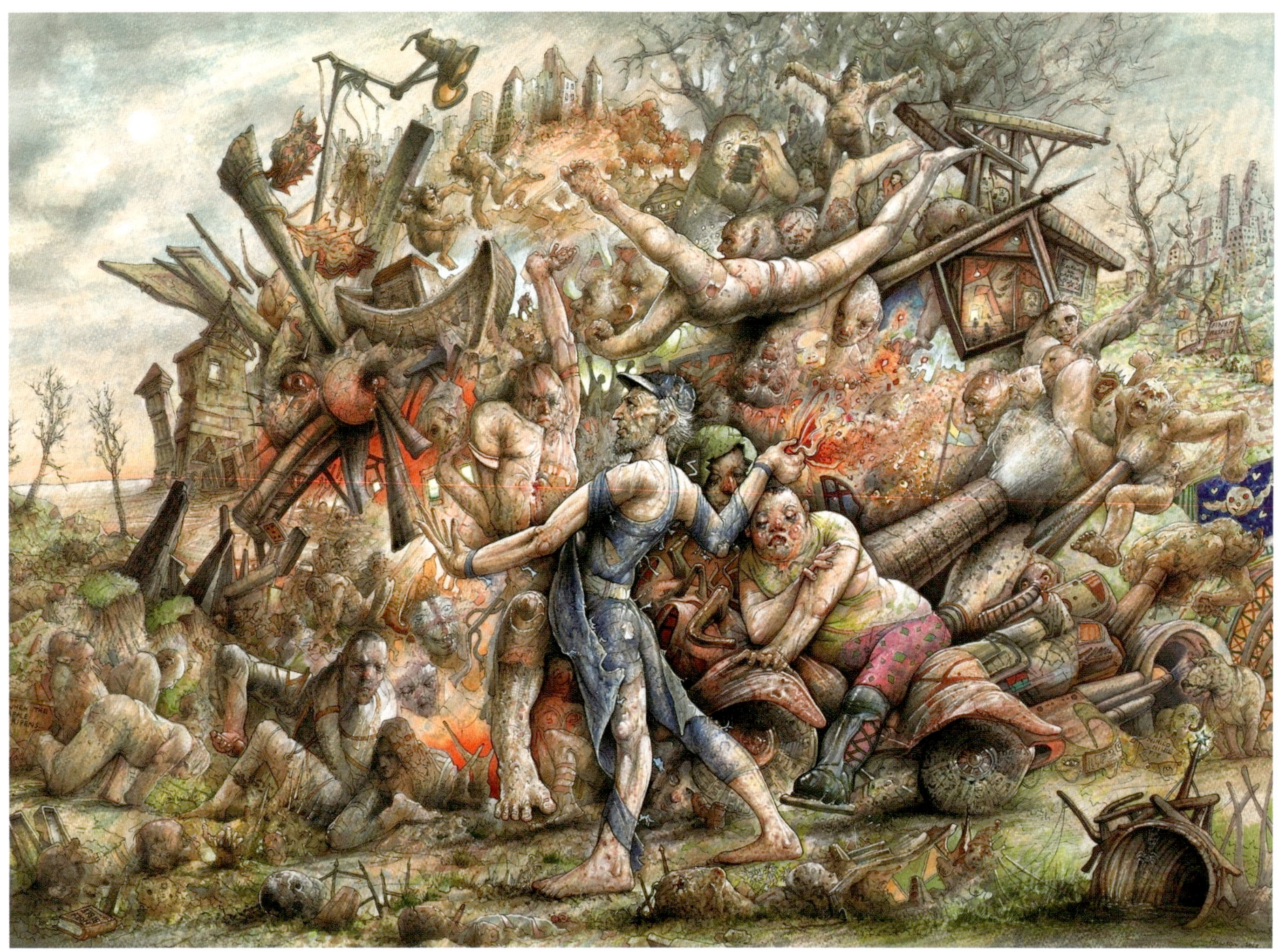

Impare Marti (With Mars Unequal)
2022 / inks on paper / 51 x 76 cm
private collection / photograph Ian Marshall

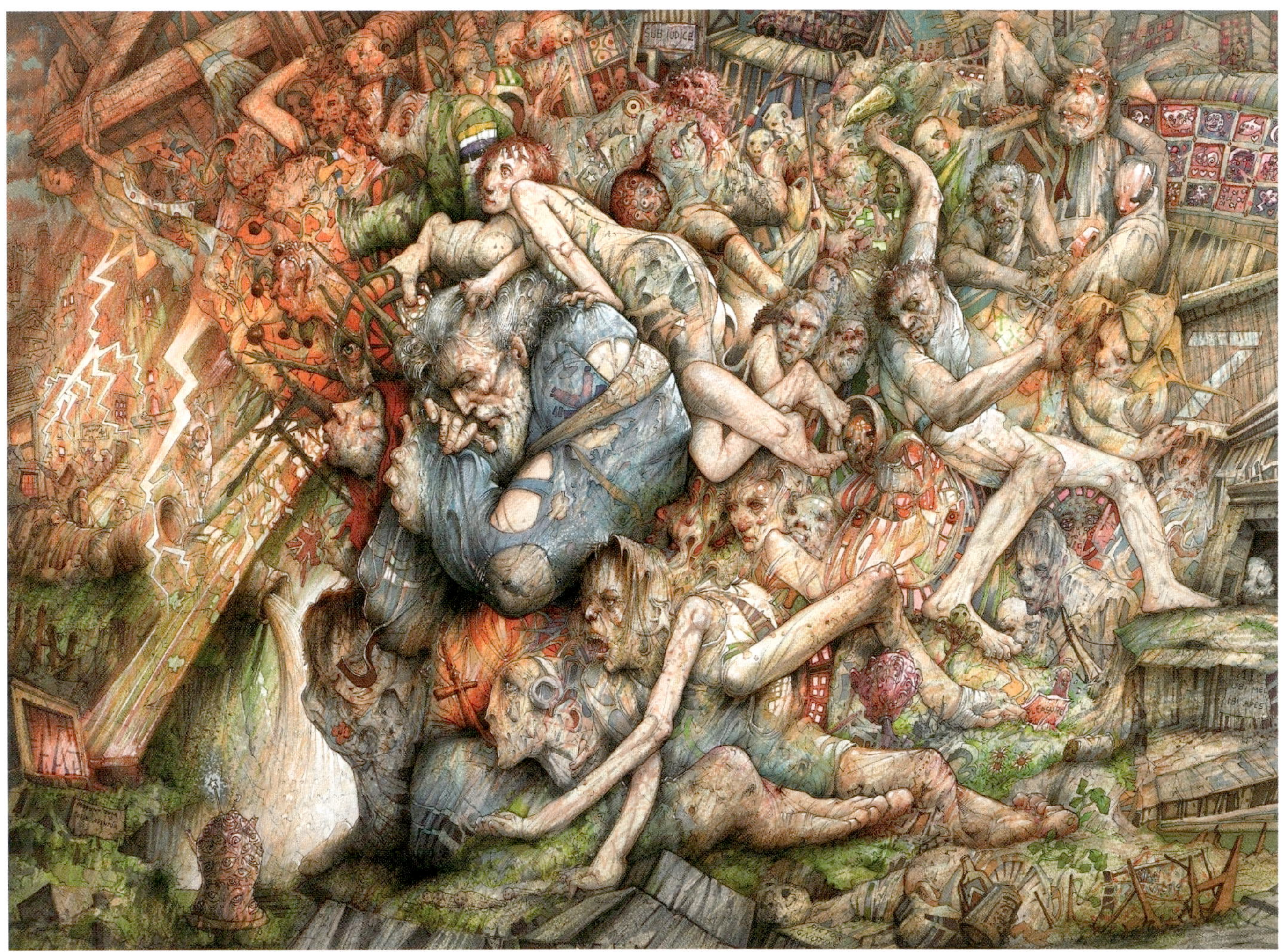

Insanus Omnis Furere Credit Ceteros (All Madmen Think That Everyone Else Is Mad)
2022 / inks on paper / 51 x 76 cm
private collection / photograph Ian Marshall

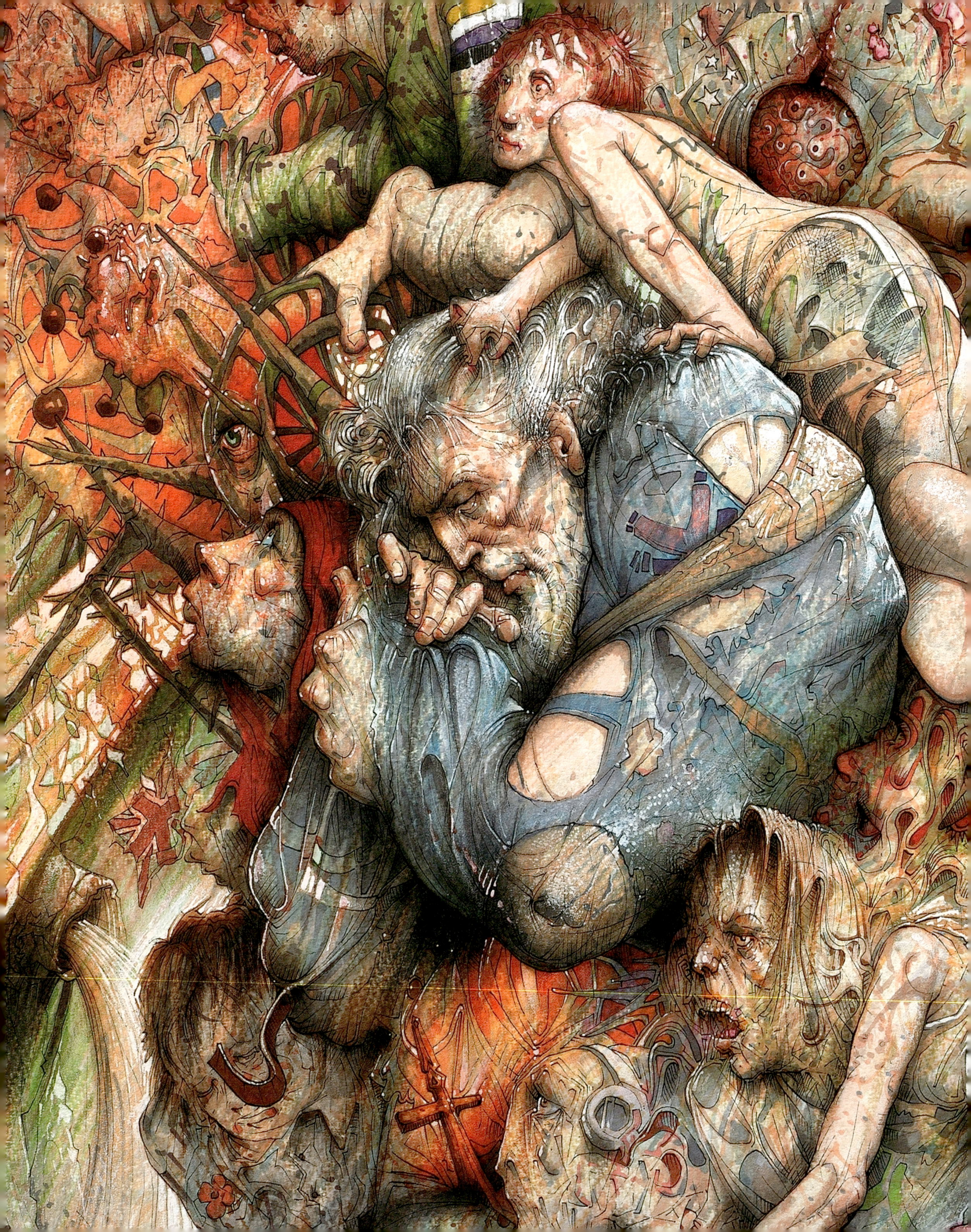

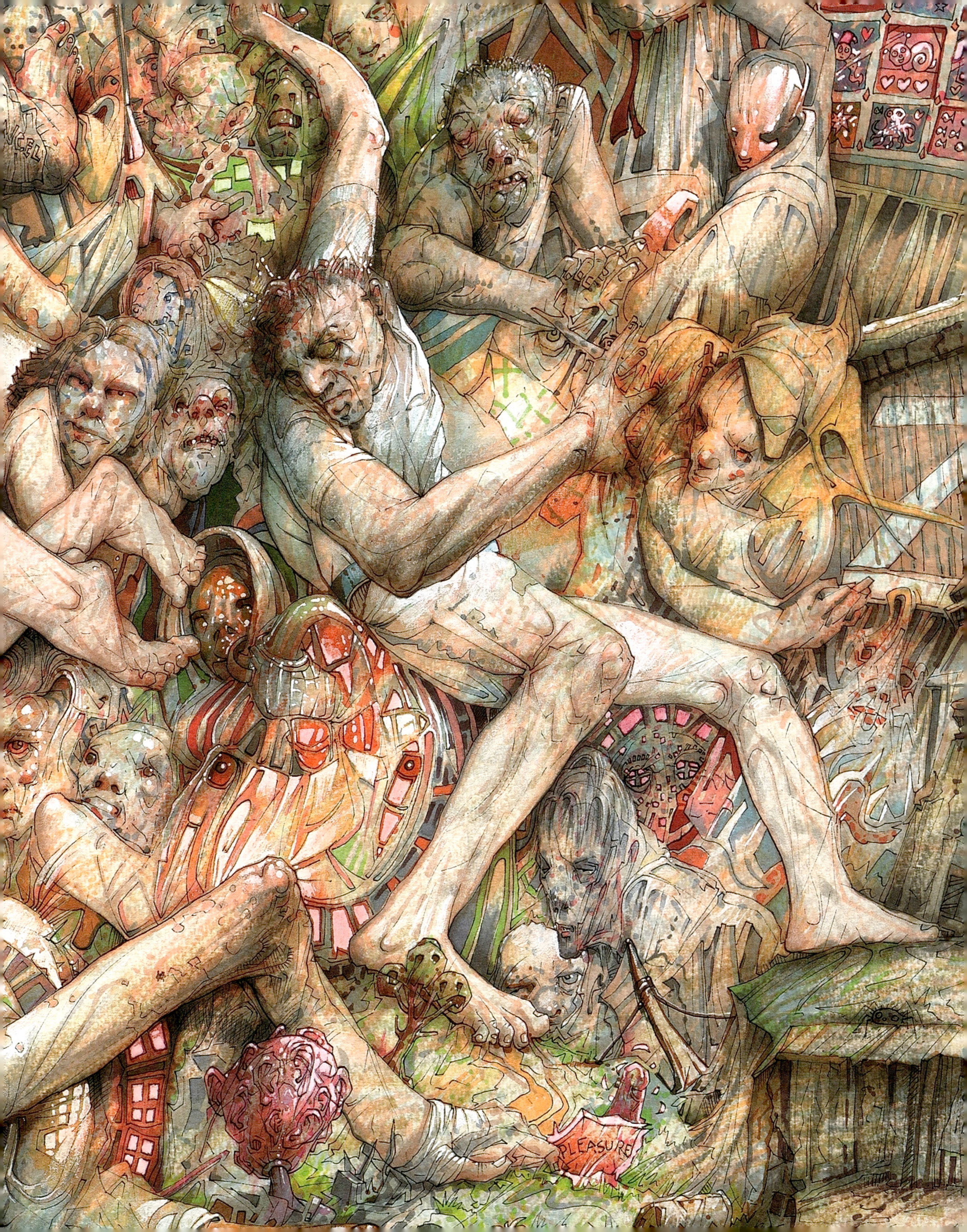

PLEASURE
PLEASURE

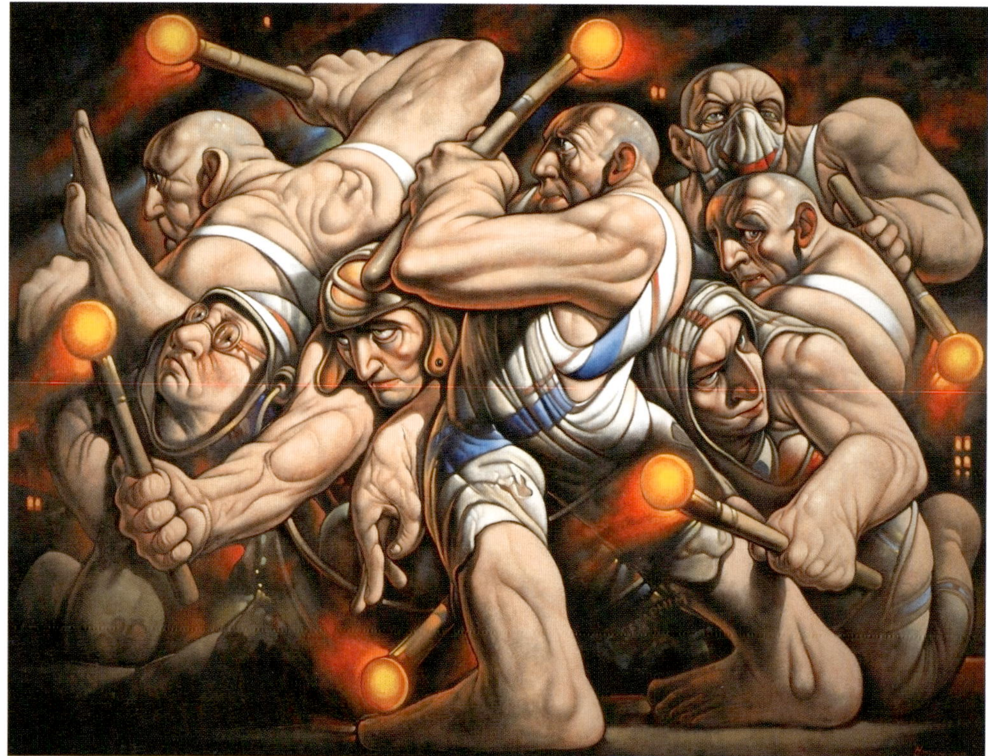

Wagner
2023 / oil on canvas / 183 x 244 cm
Flowers Gallery / photograph Ian Marshall

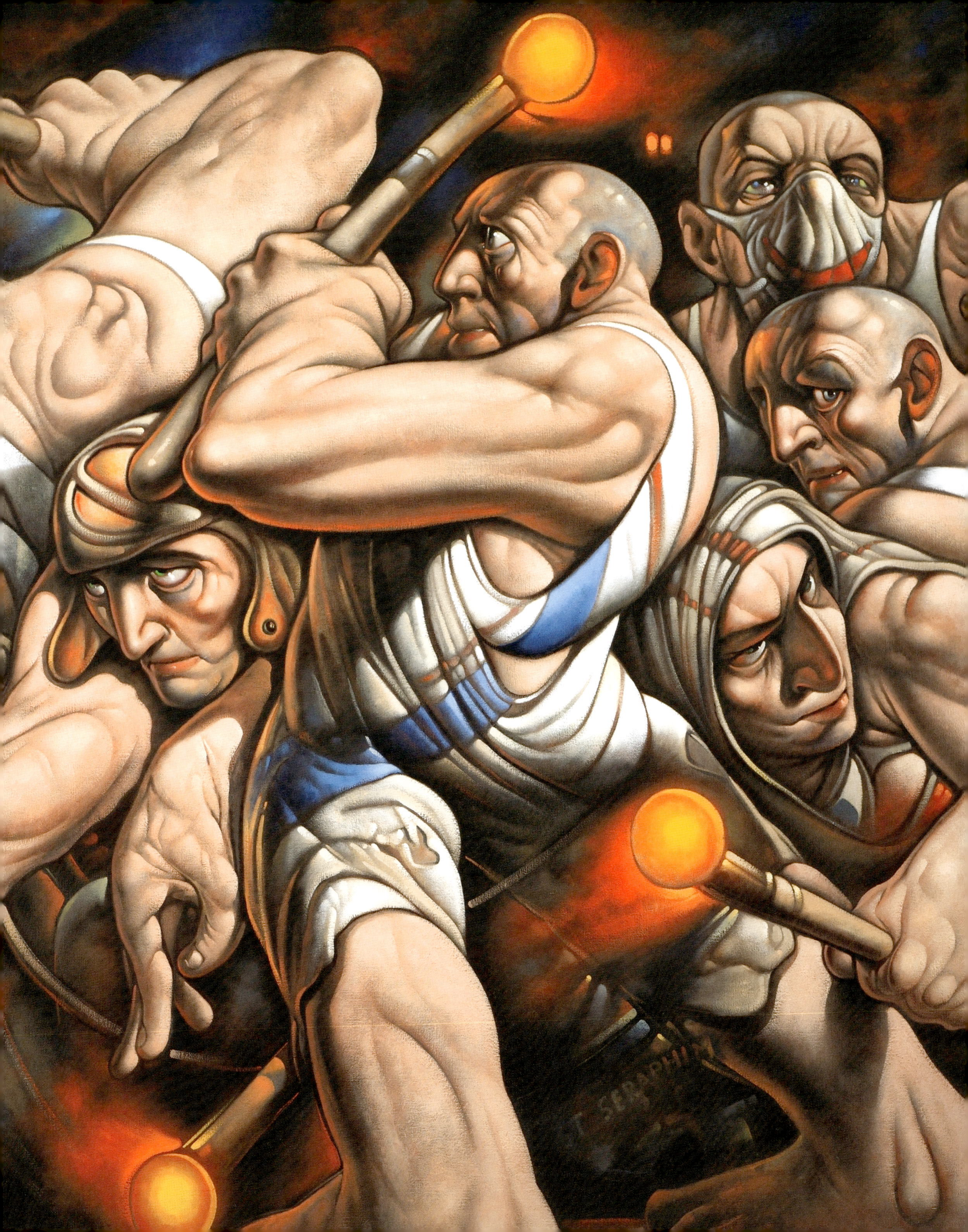

PETER HOWSON

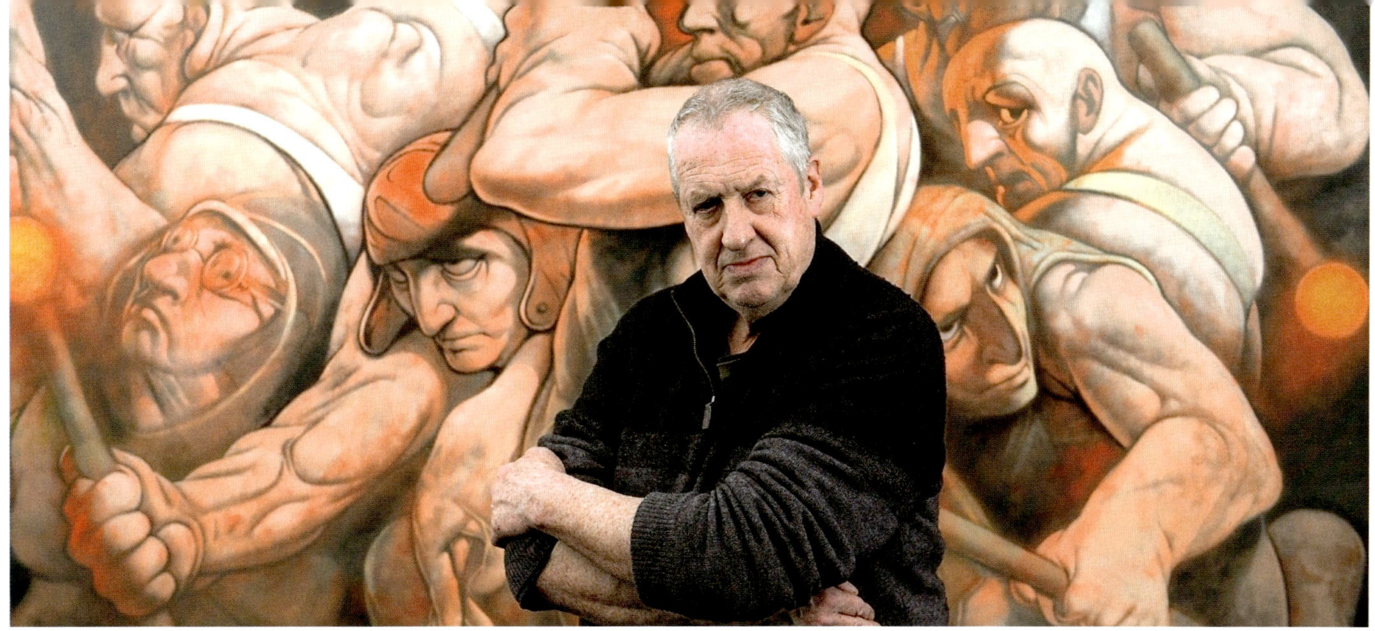

Born 1958, London

Education
1985 • Artist in Residence, University of St Andrews
1979–81 • Glasgow School of Art
1971–75 • Glasgow School of Art

Awards and honours
2009 • Appointed OBE by Her Majesty Queen Elizabeth II
1996 • Awarded Doctor of Letters Honoris Causa,
University of Strathclyde
1995 • Lord Provost's Medal, Glasgow
1993 • Appointed Official British War Artist for Bosnia
1992 • Eastward Publication Prize, RGI [Royal Glasgow
Institute], McLellan Galleries; Glasgow Nomination
for Lord Provost Prize at RGI, McLellan Galleries;
Glasgow European Young Artists Prize, Sophia,
Belgrade
1988 • Henry Moore Foundation Prize
1986 • Prize winner, Scottish Drawing Competition;
Paisley Art Galleries Arthur Andersen & Co.
Purchase Prize; Glasgow Edwin Morgan
Artists Prize
1979 • Hospitalfield Scholarship

Exhibitions
Exhibition year-dates given show the year in which
an exhibition, or the first exhibition of a tour, opened,
and not the full extent of the exhibition's run.

Selected solo ehibitions
2022 • *Lacrimae Rerum*, Flowers Hong Kong
2021 • *Phlegethon*, Flowers Cork Street, London;
Baird Institute, Cumnock, East Ayrshire,
Scotland

2020 • *When the World Changed: The Lockdown
Drawings*, Flowers, online
2019 • *The Massacre of Srebrenica*, St Mungo Museum
of Religious Life and Art, Glasgow; *Mà Vlàst*,
Roger Billcliffe Gallery, Glasgow
2018 • *Acta Est Fabula*, Flowers Kingsland Road, London;
Devils Chorus, Maclaurin Art Gallery, Ayrshire,
Scotland
2017 • *Spiritus Mundi*, Roger Billcliffe Gallery, Glasgow;
Prophecy, Flowers New York, New York
2016 • *Babylon*, Maclaurin Art Gallery, Ayrshire, Scotland
2015 • *Demokratia*, Flowers Kingsland Road, London
2013 • *From Death to Life*, Maclaurin Art Gallery,
Ayrshire, Scotland
2012 • *Redemption*, Flowers New York, New York
2011 • Saint John Ogilvie, St Andrew's Cathedral,
Glasgow
2010 • *Tilting at Windmills*, Flowers Kingsland Road,
London; *Night of the Soul*, Flowers Cork Street,
London
2009 • *Famine*, St Mungo Museum of Religious Life
and Art, Glasgow
2008 • *Harrowing of Hell*, Flowers East, London
2006 • *Andrew: Portrait of a Saint*, City Art Centre,
Edinburgh; *Peter Howson: Retrospective*,
Kunstverein, Lingen, Germany; *The Last Supper*,
Carby Art Gallery, Aberdeen
2005 • *Christos Anneste*, Flowers New York, New York;
Peter Howson: New Works, Flowers East, London
2004 • *Inspired by the Bible*, New College, Edinburgh;
Stations of the Cross, St Mary's Cathedral,
Glasgow
2003 • *Stations of the Cross*, Flowers East, London
2002 • *The Third Step*, Maclaurin Art Gallery, Ayrshire,
Scotland; Flowers Central, London

2001 • Flowers West, Los Angeles
2000 • Roger Billcliffe Gallery, Glasgow; Royal Glasgow Institute, Glasgow
1999 • Roger Billcliffe Gallery, Glasgow; *Sex, War, and Religion*, Flowers East, London
1998 • Art Institute of Southern California; *World Cup: Football Paintings*, Gallery M, London; Flowers West, Los Angeles; *Football Paintings*, Roger Billcliffe Gallery, Glasgow; *New Paintings, Drawings and Prints*, Flowers East, London
1997 • *New Work*, Flowers East, London; Djanogly Art Gallery, University of Nottingham
1996 • *The Rake's Progress and Other Paintings*, Flowers East, London; Drawing and Art Association of Norway, Oslo, *Cabinet Paintings*, Roger Billcliffe Gallery, Glasgow; Drumcroon Education Art Centre, Wigan
1994 • *Bosnia*, Imperial War Museum London, and Flowers East, London; *Bosnian Harvest*, Glasgow Print Studio, Glasgow
1993 • *The Common Man*, Flowers East, London; *A Retrospective*, McLellan Galleries, Glasgow; *The Lowland Heroes and Other Drawings*, Flowers East, London
1992 • Galería Estiarte, Madrid
1991 • *New Prints*, Flowers Graphics, London; *New Paintings*, Lannon-Cole Gallery, Chicago; *The Blind Leading the Blind*, Flowers East, London; *Recent Paintings and Drawings*, Maclaurin Art Gallery, Ayrshire, Scotland
1990 • *Drawings and Small Paintings*, Agarte, Rome; *Mayfest Exhibition*, Glasgow Print Studio, Glasgow; Los Angeles International Art Exposition
1989 • *Saracen Heads*, Flowers Graphics, London; *Paintings and Drawings*, Flowers East, London; *New Prints*, Flowers Graphics, London; *Drawings*, Tegnerforbundet, Norway
1988 • *New Works on Paper*, The Scottish Gallery, Edinburgh; *Small Works on Paper*, The Scottish Gallery, Edinburgh; *Small Paintings and Works on Paper*, Angela Flowers Gallery, London; *The Twilight Zone*, Cleveland Gallery, Middlesbrough; Quay Arts Centre, Isle of Wight
1987 • Washington Gallery, Glasgow; Angela Flowers Gallery, London
1985 • *New Paintings and Drawings*, Mayfest, Glasgow Print Studio; *New Paintings*, Crawford Centre for the Arts, University of St Andrews
1983 • *Wall Murals*, Feltham Community Association, London

Selected group exhibitions
2022 • *Head to Head*, GBS Fine Art, Wells, Somerset
2021 • *Bosnian Twilight (The Silent Forest)*, Kelvingrove Art Gallery and Museum, Glasgow
2020 • The Ingram Collection: *Collector's Favourites*, online; *Isolation: Solitary, Suspended*, Flowers, online
2019 • *Radical Drawing*, Herbert Art Gallery & Museum, Coventry; *Reflection: British Art in an Age of Change*, Ferens Art Gallery, Hull
2017 • *Ink*, Glasgow Print Studio, Glasgow
2016 • *Art of War*, Perth Art Gallery, Scotland
2015 • *Caught in the Crossfire*, Guildford House Gallery
2014 • *Reflections of War*, Flowers Kingsland Road, London; *Spheres of Influence II*, Reid Gallery; *Scottish Figuration*, Flowers Cork Street, London
2013 • *Stranger: An Exhibition of Self-Portraits*, Flowers Kingsland Road, London
2007 • *The Apprentice*, Spectrum, London; *John Lennon*

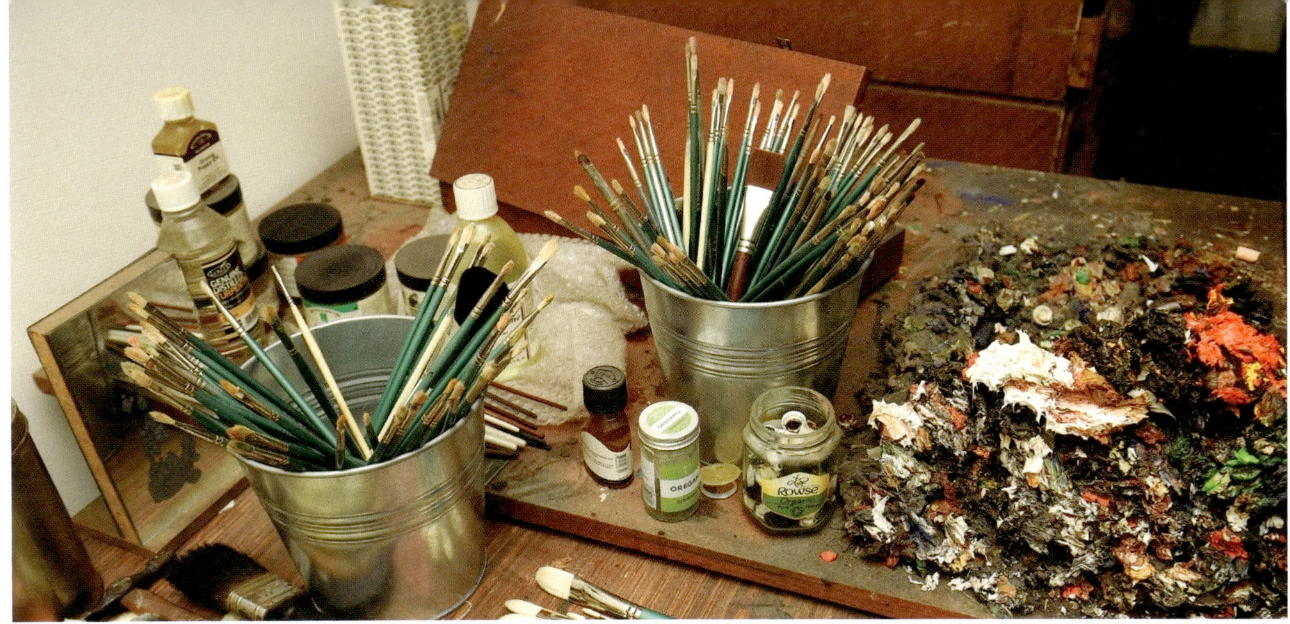

Northern Lights Festival, Durness, Sutherland,
Scotland

2005 • 35th Anniversary Exhibition, Flowers East,
London

2004 • *Presence*, St Paul's Cathedral, London;
Contemporary Nudes, Flowers East, London;
Howson and Hirst, Discerning Eye Exhibition,
Mall Galleries, London

2003 • *The New Glasgow Boys*, The Fleming Collection,
London

2001 • *12 British Figurative Painters*, Flowers West,
Los Angeles

2000 • *30th Anniversary Exhibition*, Flowers East,
London; *Wild Tigers of Bandhavgarh*, The Burrell
Collection, Glasgow; *Labour Intensive: Howson
and Herman*, The City Gallery, Leicester

1999 • *Post Impressions*, British Library, London;
Contemporary British Landscape, Flowers East,
London

1998 • The Lord Provost's Prize 1998, Gallery of Modern
Art, Glasgow; *Self-Portrait*, Six Chapel Row
Gallery, Bath

1997 • *Art et Guerre*, Galerie Piltzer, Paris; *After the
War Was Over*, Angela Flowers Ireland, Co. Cork;
The Body Politic, Wolverhampton Art Gallery,
Wolverhampton

1996 • *Naked*, Flowers East, London; *Wheels on Fire:
Cars in Art, 1950–1996*, Wolverhampton Art
Gallery; *Realism*, Künstlersonderbund in
Deutschland, Gropius Bau, Berlin; *Four British
Painters*, John McEnroe Gallery, New York; *Four
British Painters*, Mendenhall Gallery, California

1995 • *Message from Bosnia: Peter Howson and Iain
McColl*, Dick Institute, Kilmarnock, and touring;
25th Anniversary Exhibition, Flowers East, London;

Flowers at Koplin, Koplin Gallery, Los Angeles

1994 • *Inner Visions*, Flowers East, London

1993 • Nottingham Castle Museum and Art Gallery,
Nottingham

1992 • *Artist's Choice*, Flowers East, London; *Portrait
of the Artist's Mother Done from Memory*,
Flowers East, London; *Figure in the City*,
Talbot Rice Gallery, Edinburgh; Galerie Mia
Joosten, Amsterdam; The New Civic Theatre
Gallery, Maastricht; Y'Art and P. Gallery, Utrecht;
BP Gallery, Brussels; *Innocence and Experience*,
Manchester City Art Gallery, Ferens Art Gallery,
Hull

1991 • Flowers East, London; *The Boat Show*,
Smiths Galleries, London; *Inaugural Exhibition*,
Lannon-Cole Gallery, Chicago; *Human*, Suburban
Fine Arts Center, Chicago

1990 • *Flowers at Moos: Faulkner, Howson, Jones,
Keane, Kirby, Waller*, Galerie Moos, New York;
21 Years of Contemporary Art, Compass Gallery,
Glasgow; *Edinburgh Salutes Glasgow*, The
Scottish Gallery, Edinburgh; *Glasgow's Great
British Art Exhibition*, McLellan Galleries, Glasgow;
Old Museum of Transport, Glasgow; *Three
Generations of Scottish Painters*, Beaux Arts, Bath;
John Bellany, Peter Howson, Jock McFadyen,
Pamela Auchincloss Gallery, New York

1989 • *Angela Flowers Gallery 1970–1990*, Barbican
Concourse Gallery, London; *Big Paintings*,
Flowers East, London; *Confrontation: Three
British Painters*, Joy Emery Gallery, Michigan;
*Picturing People: Figurative Painting from
Britain 1945–89*, Kuala Lumpur, Hong Kong and
Singapore (touring exhibition); *4th International
Young Artists Competition*, Sofia, Bulgaria

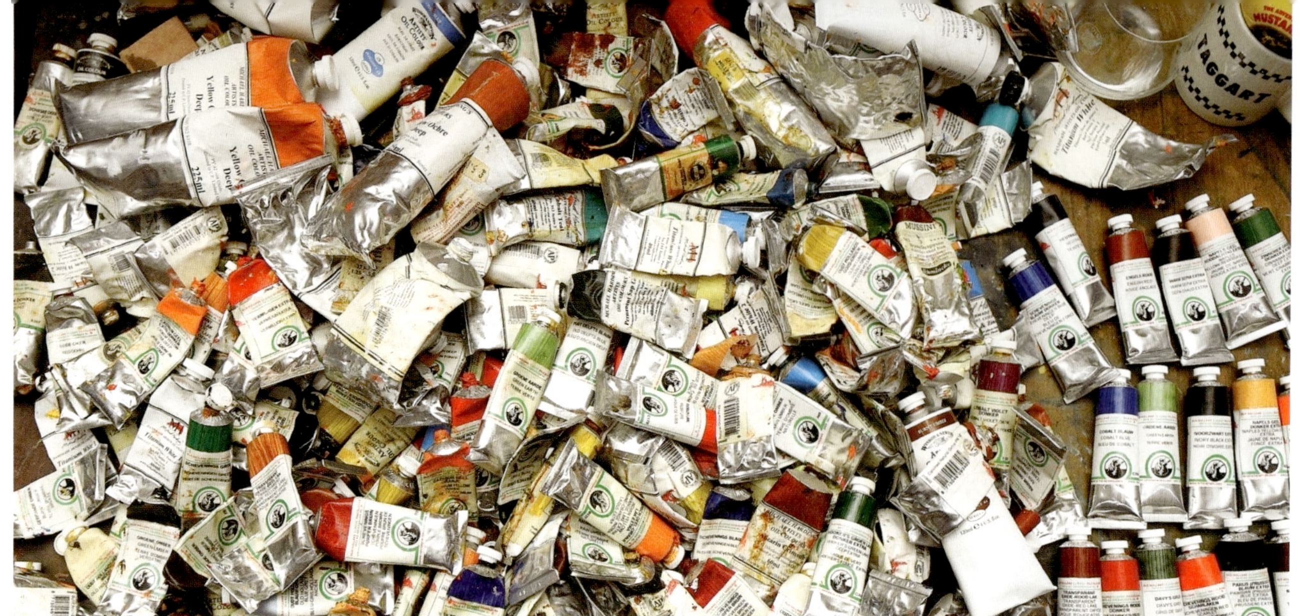

1988 • *Contemporary Portraits*, Flowers East, London; *Figure II: Naked*, Aberystwyth Arts Centre; *The New British Painting*, Contemporary Arts Center, Cincinnati (touring exhibition)

1987 • *Eighty, European Painters*, Europe (touring exhibition); *Scottish Contemporary Paintings*, Turberville Smith Gallery, London; *Critical Realism*, Nottingham Castle Museum and Art Gallery, Nottingham; *The Vigorous Imagination*, Scottish National Gallery of Modern Art; *Passage West*, Angela Flowers Ireland, Co. Cork

1986 • *New Art from Scotland*, The Warwick Arts Trust, London; *New Work* (with Stephen Barclay), Paton Gallery, London; *The Barras*, Mayfest exhibition, Compass Gallery, Glasgow; *The Eye of the Storm: Scottish Artists and the Nuclear Arms Debate*, The Stirling Smith Art Gallery and Museum, Stirling (touring exhibition); *Scottish Art Today: Artists at Work 1986*, Edinburgh International Festival

1985 • *Networking*, O'Kane Gallery, Houston, Texas; *New Image Glasgow*, Third Eye Centre, Glasgow; Air Gallery, London (and touring elsewhere); *Unique and Original*, Glasgow Print Studio (touring exhibition); *The Smith Biennale*, The Stirling Smith Art Gallery and Museum, Stirling; *Five Scottish Artists*, Leinster Fine Art, London

1984 • *Winning Hearts and Minds*, Transmission Gallery, Glasgow

1983 • *Three Scottish Artists*, Maclaurin Art Gallery, Ayrshire, Scotland; *Grease and Water: The Art and Technique of Lithography*, Printmaker's Workshop, Edinburgh

1982 • *Pictures of Ourselves*, Scottish Arts Council Travelling Gallery

1981 • *Naked Nude*, 369 Gallery, Edinburgh

Public collections

Aberdeen Art Gallery
Aberystwyth University
Arts Council England
Bankfield Museum, Halifax
British Broadcasting Corporation
British Council
British Museum, London
Calouste Gulbenkian Museum Modern Collection, Lisbon
Cartwright Hall Art Gallery, Bradford
Christie's Corporate Collection
City Art Centre, Edinburgh
Contemporary Art Society
Creative Scotland
East Ayrshire Leisure Trust CollectionsÉigse Carlow Arts Festival Collection
Fitzwilliam Museum, Cambridge
Glasgow Museums (Kelvingrove Art Gallery and Museum)
Glasgow Royal Concert Hall
The Hunterian, Glasgow
Imperial War Museum London
Isle of Man Arts Council
Library of Congress, Washington DC
Lloyds Banking Group, London
Maclaurin Trust, Ayr
The McManus: Dundee's Art Gallery and Museum
Metropolitan Museum of Art, New York
Ministry of Defence, London
Museum of Modern Art, New York
National Museum [Norway], Oslo
New York Public Library
Nottingham Castle Museum and Art Gallery, Nottingham
Paisley Museum and Art Galleries
Pallant House Gallery, Chichester
People's Palace, Glasgow

Peter Scott Gallery, Lancaster University, Lancaster
Robert Fleming Merchant Bank, London
Royal Bank of Scotland
Scottish Amicable
Scottish Enterprise
Scottish National Gallery of Modern Art, Edinburgh
Scottish Television (STV)
Southampton City Art Gallery
Tate, London
University of Strathclyde, Glasgow
University of Utah, Salt Lake City
Victoria and Albert Museum, London
Walker Art Gallery, Liverpool
Yale Center for British Art, New Haven

ACKNOWLEDGEMENTS

THE CONTRIBUTORS

Peter Howson would like to thank: David Patterson and the staff at the City Art Centre for hosting the exhibition and the related events programme. Susan Mansfield for her insightful essay, and to Sansom and Company for the time and effort they have put into publishing this book.

Matthew Flowers for his essay contribution, and to the staff at Flowers Gallery in London for their ongoing support. Heartfelt thanks to the many private and public lenders who have been willing to lend paintings to this retrospective. I am deeply grateful.

Finally, to my Studio Manager Stan Bethwaite for his guidance and dedication.

Matthew Flowers is a London-based contemporary art dealer, directing Flowers Gallery since the 1980s – the decade when the gallery started representing Peter. Throughout his career he has been on the boards of international art fairs, arts institutions and charities, championing arts education and artists' rights. Representing international living artists and estates through its London, Hong Kong and New York bases, his gallery has staged more than 900 exhibitions and is a publisher of artist editions and monographs. A former professional musician, Flowers is also a keyboardist and competitive chess player.

Susan Mansfield is a writer and journalist who has been writing widely about the arts and literature in Scotland for nearly thirty years. A features and arts writer for *The Scotsman* from 2001 until 2013, she was shortlisted for Interviewer of the Year at the Scottish Press Awards. Susan has been an art critic for *The Scotsman* since 2007. She is also a poet and playwright and was the joint winner of the Jack Clemo National Poetry Award in 2018. Her books include *The Great Tapestry of Scotland: The Making of a Masterpiece* (2013), and *Victoria Crowe: 50 Years of Painting* (2019).

David Patterson is Curatorial and Conservation Manager with Edinburgh Museums and Galleries, based at the City Art Centre. He was formerly curator of fine art, responsible for the management and development of the City of Edinburgh's 'Recognized' collection of Scottish art. He has over thirty years of exhibition curation experience, and has originated and toured exhibitions throughout the UK, Europe and to New Zealand. This is his second exhibition with Peter.